Special Education Referral or Not

Using Data to Determine Between Interventions and Referral

A Practical Resource (not a Theory Book)

Steve Gill and Ushani Nanayakkara

All Rights reserved by Steve Gill and Ushani Nanayakkara

All Rights reserved by Steve Gill and Ushani Nanayakkara

Acknowledgments

The authors would like to thank Steve's colleagues and friends, Rani Bauer, Martin Wu, Keith Mars, Barbara Abbott, Vandy Lehtonen, and Patty Finnegan, for their time and thoughtful input into this book.

A special thank you to Keith Mars and Ushani Nanayakkara. Keith was Steve's School Psychologist Internship Supervisor. Steve had always struggled greatly with writing skills, and received little teaching on how to write well through high school, undergraduate, and graduate school studies. Keith took a great deal of time to help Steve become a better writer. Also a special thank you from Steve to Ushani. Steve's drafts are written for an audience of school psychologists and special education experts. Ushani does a great job making the material more applicable to a wider audience.

All Rights reserved by Steve Gill and Ushani Nanayakkara

Table of Contents

Preface 7
   The Purpose of This Book 7
   Analysis Matrix 8
   This Book Is Not 9
   This Book Is 9

Chapter 1: Introduction 11
   Some of the Problems in This Field 11
      Structure of the Book 12
      Don't Use the "R" Word Unless You Really Mean It… 13
      Disproportionality 14
      Applicable Laws and the Issues that Arise from Those Laws 15
   A Belief of the Authors 18
   Special Education Qualification Rates in Washington State 19

Chapter 2: LE^{3}AP 22
   The Process of Evaluating Critical Data 26
   Analysis Matrix 31

Chapter 3: Data Analysis 32
   Do You Know Your School and District Data? 32
   How to Analyze School and District Data to Help Make Better Decisions 34

Chapter 4: Intervention Focused Examples 38

Chapter 5: Referral Focused Examples 53

Chapter 6: Belief Systems 67
      Our Personal Journey 67
      1. We See What We Are Acculturated To See 69

All Rights reserved by Steve Gill and Ushani Nanayakkara

2. Steve's Personal Educator Journey: The painful life lessons 72

3. Steve Hirsch's Research 74

4. Monolingual Nation: Our Expectations of Our Students 76

5. Literacy and Intelligence 78

6. Poverty 79

7. Qualification vs Disability 80

8. Reading and Referrals 82

9. Impact of Race on Qualification Rates 89

"Takeaways" 92

Closing Thoughts On Belief Systems 94

Chapter 7: Examples for Special Education Evaluation Reports 96

Chapter 8: Special Education Categories: Problem areas 112

Chapter 9: Face Validity 129

Appendix A: Sources of Information Regarding Problems in Qualification 137

Appendix B: Recommended Books 143

Appendix C: Training by Steve Gill 144

All Rights reserved by Steve Gill and Ushani Nanayakkara

Preface

The Purpose of This Book

This book is a product of many discussions we have had over several years. These discussions began with our first book *The ELL Critical Data Process,* during training sessions on the ELL Critical Data Process, and continued with our second book *Evaluating ELL Students for the Possibility of Special Education Qualification.* Educators were looking for a process that can be used with all students, not just for ELL students. This led us to put together this workbook. We took the "ELL" aspects out of the Matrix Process, and created a similar process for use with students in general. The ELL Critical Data Process is the better choice for ELL students, since it covers items that are specific to language acquisition.

Our first book, *The ELL Critical Data Process,* is a resource book, with the focus on providing educators the ELL Critical Data Process and helping them understand how to complete the process. The second book, *Evaluating ELL Students for the Possibility of Special Education Qualification,* is also a resource book, and it helps educators increase the accuracy of their special education evaluations of English Language Learners. It also has more general content to help address issues that are caused by belief systems.

Special Education Referral or Not is also meant to be a resource book. In this book we provide educators with a matrix based process for analyzing the data for non-ELL students and for determining whether more interventions or a special education referral is the appropriate next step. This book is not a manual on how to process a special education referral from the legal/procedural standpoint, but instead focuses on helping teams process data that is critical to the decision-making process during a special education referral or prior to a special education referral.

All three books are workbooks, intended to be resources for educators; they are not books about theories on these issues.

All Rights reserved by Steve Gill and Ushani Nanayakkara

Analysis Matrix

The Matrix Process is about collecting the most critical data, gathering the key staff members, and having the crucial discussions to understand what each piece of data is indicating. The matrix helps teams focus their discussion and record their impressions of the meaning of each piece of data which can range from more intervention, to neutral, to the need for a special education referral.

The following is the matrix that staff complete while analyzing their data.

	1	2	3	4	5	6	7	8	9	10	11	12	13	14
Data supports referral										■		■		
Between Neutral and Supports Referral										■		■		
Neutral														
Between Neutral and More Interventions								■						
Data supports more intervention(s)								■						

This process guides educators through a practical process that will lead to the visual representation of their discussions within the matrix. This provides staff a way to understand whether more interventions are needed or if a special education referral is the appropriate next step.

All Rights reserved by Steve Gill and Ushani Nanayakkara

This Book Is Not

This book does not replace:

- District policy and/or practice in your area, unless your district adopts some or all of these concepts.
- State law requirements for your state.
- Your requirement to collect all pertinent data during the referral process.

This book is not an extensive review of literature with a series of quotes to be interpreted by the reader. The quotes used in this workbook are meant to be reused by educators when they challenge the belief systems of others who are creating or maintaining the systems that lead to disproportionate results. Remember, though, that these are good people, with good intentions, who need education, not criticism, even if they are achieving poor results. We can all benefit from looking at our results and examining our practices, acculturation and belief systems to understand the root causes of our results (we are good people, even if we are getting poor results, and the problems are subtle problems, not outright actions with malice). With good results we need to know what to continue and with poor results we need to know what to change.

This Book Is

The purpose of this workbook is to:

- Provide you and your team a straightforward method for collecting and analyzing critical data that is part of the special education referral process.
- Provoke thinking about the impact of exposure, experience, expectations, and practice on presenting problems.
- Assist teams in building their processes.

All Rights reserved by Steve Gill and Ushani Nanayakkara

- Reduce over identification of students who struggle as students in need of special education by understanding what the most appropriate intervention is for the student.
- Help teams understand children as individuals (this will make more sense later, so please don't take offense).

Our goal is to make sure we are helping students to receive the services they need to be successful, to only qualify students for special education who truly have a disability that impacts their ability to access their education, and who need a specially designed instruction directly correlated to the disability and its adverse impact.

Remember:

- Not all kids who struggle have disabilities, even if they are performing well below expected levels.
- Not all kids with disabilities need special education (specially designed instruction). Some might need 504 plans (accommodations and/or modifications, but not specially designed instruction), some might not need either.
- We tend to over qualify, not under qualify (you will find evidence of that later in the book). We need to keep this in mind as we examine our data.

Chapter 1: Introduction

Some of the Problems in This Field

After a short introduction this workbook starts with the Matrix Process for assessing students, then provides other critical information educators need to be successful in working with their teams and their own belief systems. If you want to jump straight into the meat of the process, go ahead and skip to Chapter 2 for right now, but do come back to read the introduction. The job of processing referrals is a difficult and stressful job, even with good people wanting to do a good job. The data from schools with strong RTI/MTSS programs show us that we test and qualify far too many children (RTI is Response to Intervention and MTSS is Multi-Tiered Systems of Support). After spending time on the chapters that focus on the Matrix Process make sure to process all of the chapters equally.

Education is possibly the field of work that takes the longest to react to research and implement changes. A large part of this, in the authors' opinion, is due to subtle belief systems. If you would like to read research that supports this opinion, Dan C. Lortie was one of the first researchers in this area and others have agreed with his key findings.

Since beginning in the field of school psychology, Steve has read many books and papers about what one should and should not do, but nothing that makes the process significantly better than a guessing game for many of the more challenging cases. This problem is most prevalent with students who might qualify under the category of Specific Learning Disability. The previous statement might bother some people, until they examine the research on the impact of RTI/MTSS, the impact of short intensive interventions, and the research on the effectiveness of current SLD identification. The goal of this workbook is to reduce the likelihood that a practitioner will be guessing at the end of the evaluation. Please note, some practitioners currently believe that what they are doing is solid practice, even though their practices lead to extremely disproportionate rates of qualification. After working with more than 200 school districts and training over 5,000 educators, staff members, and practitioners on the ELL Critical Data Process and related ELL/Special Education issues, Steve can honestly state that not a single district he has worked with actually knew their disproportionality issues beyond the most superficial of levels. Few educators know that the Specific Learning Disability category tripled from 1975 to 2000/2004 and accounted for 50% of all students qualified for special education services. Since then, the category of Specific Learning Disability has decreased from 50% to 39.2% and continues to drop, all while RTI/MTSS has become more prevalent.

Structure of the Book

Introduction --- Some history and brief coverage of what is to come

LE³AP --- The Matrix Process in this book is primarily for non-ELLs (however, it is also applicable to ELL students), with a focus on **L**ooking at **E**xposure, **E**xperience, **E**xpectations and **P**ractice. LE³AP will guide you through data collection and processing of the data to help you understand if more interventions are needed and what those might be, or if a special education referral is the route to take. This process provides many of the pieces you will need to complete an evaluation, if that is the decision made at the end of the process.

Intervention --- Using the collected data to understand what interventions are needed, if that is the decision of the team.

Evaluation --- Documenting the data that was produced during this process and that you will need to complete an appropriate evaluation.

School Building and District Data --- The questions that need to be answered and much of the data that needs to be collected to know where your disproportionality occurs, so that you know what challenges the team faces.

Belief Systems --- The authors and other professionals that provide training have noted that belief systems issues are some of the main reasons that disproportionality has not improved on a national level. Note that the data has not improved in a notable fashion since the beginning of measuring disproportionality. This section focuses on examples and research that help the reader understand the link between acculturation, belief systems, practices and results. Our poor results are not due to practices that are purposefully targeted at creating disproportionality, therefore the poor results are due to subtle issues within our belief systems. These subtle beliefs are created from our acculturation and lack of knowledge in certain areas.

Examples of Wording --- A section that shows how each of the factors might be worded within documents or reports for clarity and maximum impact.

Face Validity --- Creating a minimum bar regarding the data that must be collected and processed by category (hoping that the minimum exceeds what is required).

Appendices --- Information related to some of the key quotes, has Steve's biography, comments on his training, comments on Steve's and Ushani's first two books, and an overview of potential training offered by Steve.

Don't Use the "R" Word Unless You Really Mean It…

Within the schools, staff members may talk about referring a student for a special education evaluation, without really knowing what that entails. It is important to discuss the legal meaning of a referral with all staff. Do not imply that a referral needs to wait when a staff member truly wants to make a referral. Instead, help them understand that in many cases a special education evaluation is very difficult to process with accuracy when there is no history of targeted interventions. This is far more critical for students who are suspected of having a specific learning disability than it is for children with blindness. For example we rarely qualify students for special education, who have blindness, who don't really need the services that special education can provide. However, as you will see, the work by Dr. Carnine, Dr. Torgesen, and the impact of RTI/MTSS on qualification rates helps us to understand that our accuracy is not as high with students with learning disabilities.

Disproportionality

Disproportionality is common within special education and gifted/highly capable programs. In a nutshell, the students within either of these groups do not match the demographics of your school or your district. For example, if 12% of your students are Black/African American and 19% of your students are Hispanic/Latino, then within both special education and gifted/highly capable programs approximately 12% of the students should be Black/African American and approximately 19% should be Hispanic/Latino. This is not what is occurring in the vast majority of school districts, nor in any state that the authors have heard of, nor in the data for the United States as a whole. Furthermore, since the data on disproportionality has been measured, there have not been positive changes at the national level. We can either be part of maintaining this problem, making this problem worse, or be part of the solution. This book, in addition to our first two books, is meant to help you understand these problems while providing you practical actions to take in order to be part of the solution.

The following quote from the NASP Communique, Vol 38, #1, September 2009 provides evidence of the depth of these problems.

> *Black students, particularly those identified as mentally retarded or emotionally disabled, have been consistently overrepresented for more than 3 decades. Native American students are also persistently overrepresented in special education nationally, and while the same is not true for Latino students, they are often overrepresented at the state and district levels where their enrollment is highest.*

> *Special education identification patterns vary both between and within states. For instance, risk for Black students identified as mentally retarded is more than 14 times that of their White peers in some states while risk is nearly equivalent in others.*

> *The disproportionality literature tends to focus on the disability categories of mental retardation, learning disabilities, and emotional disabilities, as these are the high-incidence disabilities and constitute*

over 63% of students eligible for special education (U.S. Department of Education [USDOE], 2009). These are also widely regarded as "judgmental" categories because of relatively vague federal and state disability definitions that necessitate a high degree of professional judgment in making normative comparisons to determine eligibility (Klingner et al., 2005). This has led many to question the validity of these diagnoses as true disabilities and the likelihood of misidentification, particularly in light of the wide variation in identification rates across states and districts. In contrast, diagnoses in the low-incidence categories are rarely challenged because of their physical/medical bases, and because disproportionality is not generally observed in these categories.

Applicable Laws and the Issues that Arise from Those Laws

Our laws provide guidelines and/or requirements that we are expected to follow, yet our data clearly shows that we are not following some of these laws or that we are not looking at our data to see if our results show whether or not we are following the laws.

The laws expect that a student is not to be qualified for special education if the presenting problem can be addressed in general education with or without accommodations and modifications. Yet our results show that we have far more students receiving special education services than can be supported by data and research. Also, as RTI and MTSS have grown, specific learning disability qualification has greatly decreased.

Throughout this book the Washington Administrative Codes are used (given that the authors are in Washington State). The CFRs (federal special education laws) have the same content for each law that is noted, and all state special education laws are based upon the CFRs.

- WAC 392-172A-01035
- "Intellectual disability, a hearing impairment (including deafness), a speech or language impairment, a visual impairment (including blindness), an emotional behavioral disability, an orthopedic impairment, autism, traumatic brain injury, other health impairment, a specific learning disability, deaf-blindness, multiple disabilities, or for students, three through eight, a developmental delay and who, because of the disability and adverse educational impact, **has unique needs that cannot be addressed exclusively through education in general education classes with or without individual accommodations,** and needs special education and related services."

Bold was added for effect. This wording was added in Washington state law.

The Washington State law clearly states that a child is not to be found eligible for something that can be addressed within the general education setting. Therefore, if the school is implementing targeted interventions and those interventions are working, then the student (in almost all cases) should not be considered for or qualified for special education. The CFRs are not as bold on this statement, yet there are many indications in the CFRs that the same expectation is to be met.

Furthermore, the laws regarding appropriate instruction and language acquisition add another set of factors that must be addressed. We are supposed to be able to rule out a lack of appropriate instruction in reading and/or math, and limited English proficiency.

One last important note to this law is the following. Confusion occurs with staff around the concept of "adverse impact" and the words adverse impact. The concept "adverse impact" is about how a disability is creating an adverse impact on the child's ability to access their education and that requires special education services. The confusion is that these children are doing poorly in school. Therefore, staff have often related the words adverse impact to the concept "adverse impact" by thinking that adverse impact is synonymous with doing poorly in school. However, doing poorly in school could be related to the many other issues discussed in this book, and could have no relationship to a disability.

All Rights reserved by Steve Gill and Ushani Nanayakkara

- WAC 392-172A-03040
- "(2)(a) A student **must not be determined to be eligible** for special education services **if** the determinant factor is:

    (i) **Lack of appropriate instruction in reading**, based upon the state's grade level standards;

    (ii) **Lack of appropriate instruction in math**; or

    (iii) **Limited English proficiency**; and

   (b) If the student does not otherwise meet the eligibility criteria including presence of a disability, adverse educational impact and need for specially designed instruction.

   (3) In interpreting evaluation data for the purpose of determining eligibility for special education services, each school district must:

   (a) Draw upon information from a variety of sources, including aptitude and achievement tests, parent input, and teacher recommendations, as well as information about the student's physical condition, social or cultural background, and adaptive behavior; and

   (b) Ensure that information obtained from all of these sources is documented and carefully considered."

The issues around appropriate instruction, Limited English Proficiency, a variety of sources, and social or cultural background are all issues that often receive little or no attention within the evaluation reports for those students who have the most prevalent challenges in these areas. At times there is a great deal of pressure to "make" students eligible when staff cannot or will not recognize other issues and look for other solutions. Lack of appropriate instruction in reading and/or math is not just an ELL issue. Are the students in your school getting appropriate instruction in reading and/or math if less than 50% are passing the state tests? Or 40%? Or 30%? Or 20%?

A Belief of the Authors

There is no doubt that disproportionality in special education has existed for at least 40 years and has changed little over those 40 years. The authors believe that educators are good and caring people, because it certainly is not about the money. Knowing those two things, one must wonder why we have such discrepant numbers and results. It is the belief of the authors that we have been trained, in very subtle ways throughout our lives, to have beliefs that we are not aware of or do not know the impact of. And, with "our" we mean all of us. The problems are subtle and the most subtle of impacts of prejudice play themselves out in ways we are unaware of in our lives. The following examples can help us see our results, then maybe we will also see our practices, belief systems, and acculturation as interrelated.

The following quote was taken from a report to congress:

"Using data from the U.S. Department of Education, analyses suggest that Black children are 2.88 times more likely than White children to be labeled as having mental retardation and 1.92 times more likely to be labeled as having an emotional/behavioral disorder (Losen & Orfield, 2002). Research suggests that unconscious racial bias, stereotypes, inequitable implementation of discipline policies, and practices that are not culturally responsive may contribute to the observed patterns of identification and placement for many minority students."

Information from the *Twenty-fourth Annual Report to Congress on the Implementation of the Individuals with Disabilities Education Act (IDEA)* (U.S. Department of Education, 2002), available at:
http://www2.ed.gov/about/reports/annual/osep/2002/index.html

The later chapter on belief systems will address this at greater length and provide people with ways to examine these issues. Steve, who provides training and consultation with school districts, has experienced these issues across numerous districts. Also, Steve heard Clay Cook, a leader in MTSS work, talk about first working with districts on belief systems before working on structural issues. So, go ahead and start with the dessert (the process), but please do not forget to read and process the information on belief systems.

The following example is based on special education qualification rates in Washington State. It will help you see how much impact individuals and subtle biases can have, considering that almost all of the noted districts are extremely small school districts. The data from the following research provides a concrete example of biases impacting our practices and our results. These results demonstrate profound differences that are extremely unlikely to have happened by chance, and extremely unlikely to have happened by purposeful, harmful actions.

Special Education Qualification Rates in Washington State

Steve examined the data for 295 school districts. No district was purposely left out of the data, with the exception of school districts in the data set that were(are) not actually comprehensive school districts (e.g., School for the Blind). Therefore, with a set of 250 districts, it is highly unlikely that any district missed would have impacted the noted trends.

For 16 districts the special education eligibility qualification percentages fell below 10% of the total student population. For 15 of these 16 school districts, the average student population in the districts was 145 students (145 is the total student population and not just the total for the special education population; the 16th was a medium sized district noted separately below).

There were 32 districts with special education eligibility percentages above 18% of the total student population. The average student population across these districts was 392 students. As above, 392 represents the total student population and not just the special education population.

All Rights reserved by Steve Gill and Ushani Nanayakkara

In the State of Washington, 45.9% of the students are on Free or Reduced Lunch. The average percentage of F/R Lunch for the districts below 10% special education qualification rate was 24%. The average percentage of F/R Lunch for the districts above 18% was 75.6%.

The only medium/large district with a percentage below 10% of the student population qualified for special education services was the Issaquah School District, at 8.8%. It is interesting to note that Issaquah School District has some of the highest state test scores noted during this research.

Although the F/R Lunch difference is extreme, there is no way to prove that it is a causal factor. Yet, many research studies have indicated that poverty is a very high predictor of special education qualification. This occurs even though it would be very hard to argue, beyond a minimal percentage difference, that poverty has any correlation to rates of disabilities, and no causal relationship.

It is interesting to note that virtually all of the districts on the extremes of the range have very small student populations. In all of these cases, one or only a few people are making the qualification decisions.

It would be hard to examine this data and not see the human impact on the work. We have a lot of power in influencing outcomes, and, hopefully a lot to think about in our daily work to bring about positive student outcomes.

You will see these points repeated throughout the book because we have a very hard time seeing ourselves involved in any of the negative results ("we" being that universal we). However, most staff have not examined the data in their schools and district. We need to have the courage to look closely at our work and to begin to solve problems as they appear. The data is not the way it is because so few people are involved in the problem. Wherever there is a problem, a lot of staff members were involved in creating or maintaining the problem (remember, not bad people, just bad results). This could seem to contradict what was said above. However, in the problem noted above just a few people had "control" over the outcome, yet many people had input and involvement. So, the big "we" could have stopped the problem if they had seen it as a problem. We need as many people as possible involved in the solutions.

The research has shown that the category of Specific Learning Disability, the largest of the categories and the category frequently with the highest levels of disproportionality, is heavily impacted by human error.

More evidence of "our" impact:

- "SLD numbers may have dropped due to the proliferation of Response to Intervention (RTI)—a method of providing targeted assistance to young children who have difficulty learning—and other early-reading interventions (see *Response to Intervention*). Lastly, the identification of SLDs, though strictly outlined in policy, appears more subjective and **prone to human error** than the identification of most other disabilities; thus, SLD identification is perhaps more affected by related changes in policy, budget, personnel, etc."
- Source --- Fordham Institute Article on Trends

The words in red from the quote above (red added for emphasis), need to be challenged. School psychologists have long been described as the "gate keepers" of special education, yet Steve has found very few that like or appreciate this role. The words in red, in Steve's experience, are not quite correct. It is often not human error (an error in judgment or a mistake). For example, Steve has seen school psychologists give students two different IQ tests and two different academic tests, and then mix and match across the tests until they find a discrepancy (discrepancy model for SLD). This is not done by error. These school psychologists know that this approach is inappropriate; however, they feel a great deal of pressure by the administration and teachers to qualify students. Therefore, it is a bad choice and not a mistake/human error.

As noted above, many of us have been involved in the system that created and maintained the poor results that are so common across our nation. Now, we need to have everyone involved in the solutions.

All Rights reserved by Steve Gill and Ushani Nanayakkara

Chapter 2: LE³AP

LE³AP

Look at:

Exposure

Experience

Expectations

and

Practice

The LE³AP process takes into account these four main areas, in order to understand whether the skill deficit in question is related to Exposure/Experience/Expectations/Practice or a possible disability. In other words, once a team has looked at a problem with the "lens" of exposure, experience, expectations and practice, does the presenting problem appear (all things considered) reasonable or does it appear to represent a potential disability.

During initial trainings on the LE³AP model, many educators asked Steve how these four areas are being differentiated. For exposure, the team looks at whether or not the student was exposed to the area of concern in a manner similar to students who have learned the skill/behavior in question. Experience is differentiated by looking at whether or not the student was actively involved in the skill/behavior in question similar to students who developed the skill/behavior in question. Then, Expectation(s) is whether or not the adults in the student's environment expected them to attempt/learn the new skill/behavior (and how they supported that learning) and comparing those expectations and support with what you would normally see for a child who has learned the skill/behavior in question. Last, Practice is examining what the student (or adults) did in order to get better at the skill/behavior in question and how that compares to students who have acquired the skill/behavior in question. Practice is a focused effort on improving a skill, not solely active participation in the skill/activity (e.g., working on phoneme skills development versus pleasure reading).

It is important to note that some students do not have exposure and/or experience given that they have a disability that limited their exposure and/or experience. For a student who clearly has a medical condition that impacts their access to their education or for a student who clearly has a cognitive impairment, a process like this should be abbreviated as appropriate (based upon the documented evidence). The process might become more about data gathering for the referral and potential evaluation process (based upon facts, not impressions).

The following two examples provide some context.

Student 1:

This student was a 6th grade student who was performing well below grade level expectations. He is from a Russian background and he is one of nine siblings. The majority of his siblings were doing well in school, yet a few were doing poorly. All indicators were leading toward a special education referral. The school psychologist was in the process of interviewing the student's mother, and the information continued to support the possibility of a special education referral. Then, his mother stated, "You know he can read and write in Russian, right?" This information was not known to the team, so the school psychologist asked whether or not he could use the interpreter to get an example of his reading and writing skills.

The student came into the school psychologist's office and the school psychologist opened a webpage in Russian, asking the student to read the information and provide a summary. The student did this and provided a detailed summary, and the interpreter stated that the summary was accurate. Then, the school psychologist wrote questions in English that the interpreter did not get to see. The student wrote responses to the questions in Russian and the interpreter read these. She stated that the written responses were easy to understand, just with some misspellings. The school psychologist asked the student's mother about the family's emphasis on English versus Russian. The mother made it clear that it is very important to the family that the student learns to read and write in Russian, and that it is not so important that he reads and writes in English.

Exposure: The student has been exposed to English since very early in his life.

Experience: The student has been in an English school since Kindergarten, and was participating at a low level.

Expectations: The family expects Russian skills to be learned and mastered, not English skills.

Practice: The student had a long history of completing very little work within the school setting.

All Rights reserved by Steve Gill and Ushani Nanayakkara

Therefore, is it really reasonable to expect him to have grade level skills in English, knowing all of this???

And, a student who can read/write in their native language at a higher level than in English (with far less exposure and experience) is not a student with a learning disability.

Student 2:

A little boy or girl, 3 to 4 years of age is having a very difficult time pronouncing their words, and does not appear to even be trying. When this child wants some cereal, their mom or dad or older sibling goes to the cupboard because the child is pointing that direction and grunting. Then, they open the cupboard and the adult (or older sibling) points to the first box. The child says, "untuh." The adult or older sibling points to the second box. The child says, "untuh." Then the third box, and the child responds, "unhuh."

Exposure: It is highly likely that the child has heard all of the correct words.

Experience: The child has not been using or attempting to use the correct words.

Expectations: The adults are not expecting the child to use or attempt to use the correct words.

Practice: The child is not practicing the needed skills, whether approximations that could be shaped or the actual words.

This student could be a student with a disability or non-disability developmental delay, yet it would be very difficult to accurately assess this skill set, not knowing what some intervention and work with the family could achieve.

The following pages contain the non-ELL Matrix Process. The goal of this process is the collection of critical data, the gathering of a team of diverse educators, and then thoughtfully processing the data to understand the needs of the individual child.

All Rights reserved by Steve Gill and Ushani Nanayakkara

The Process of Evaluating Critical Data

This is a team process. Multiple team members should be involved in the data collection process: general education staff, school nurse, intervention staff and, as appropriate, special education staff.

Each of the following factors allows the team to consider its potential impact. Each team will discuss the extent to which they believe these factors impact their student and record their conclusions on the provided chart (the matrix). This provides a visual with regards to the number and severity of factors that may be impacting the student. The team should discuss and agree on the severity of the issue ranging from a need for more intervention, to neutral, to a need for a special education referral for each item. This guide gives examples of the extremes, more intervention and referral, and the teams need to discuss whether the data leads them to mark close to, or at one of those extremes, or somewhere in-between. Remember to take notes that can help in the future as evidence for designing interventions or as data in the referral and/or evaluation process.

The numbers correspond to the numbers on the matrix and the items are in the same order as on the form.

Exposure (1)--- The team needs to gather data regarding the exposure the student has had to each of the skill areas that are concerning the team. If the student has not had the same exposure to the skill area as children who have developed the skill to the expected level, then the mark should be made toward more intervention. If the student has had the expected level of exposure, similar to students who have gained the skills, and the student of concern is still not demonstrating the skills, then the mark should be made in the matrix toward referral. The team then can pick between more intervention and referral based upon their interpretation of the data for each skill, weighing exposure against skills gained.

Experience (2)--- The team, like in number 1, is trying to compare the experiences the student had with the skill of concern against the experiences of a student who is doing well developing the same skill. Exposure is simply contact with

All Rights reserved by Steve Gill and Ushani Nanayakkara

something and experience is involvement with the same thing, or direct participation. If the student directly participated in the activities needed to gain the skill(s) at the same level as students who commonly gain the skills, and the student of concern didn't gain the skills, then mark toward referral. If the student of concern did not actively participate in the activities as did the students who gained the skill(s), then mark toward more intervention.

Expectations (3)--- The team, through observation and interviews, needs to determine the expectations that have been placed upon the student regarding the skill(s) in question. Did the parent(s) or other involved adults expect the student to practice and learn the skill(s) in question? This is not a value judgment. There are times in which the adults, well meaning, will do things for students/children, because it is just easier. Low expectations lead to a mark toward more intervention and high expectations with low results lead to a mark toward referral.

Practice (4)--- The team, through observation and interviews, needs to determine the level of practice the student has had with the skill(s) in question. This is again being used to compare the student against students who have developed the skill(s) in question. If the student has not had consistent practice with the skill in question, the mark needs to be placed toward more intervention. If the student has had extensive practice with the skill(s) in question and has not demonstrated success, the mark goes toward referral. Practice needs to be a focused effort on improving a skill, not solely active participation in the skill/activity (e.g., working on phoneme skills development versus pleasure reading).

Attendance History (5)--- Any student who has three or more unexcused absences per year or a total of 15 absences per year* or more (excused or not) is outside the norm and is negatively impacted in the learning. So, place a mark in the matrix toward more intervention if they are near or above this level of absenteeism. If the student has had good attendance and is doing poorly, then place the mark in the matrix toward referral.

* This is a yearly rate, so 7-8 absences at midyear, for example, would be outside the norm.

All Rights reserved by Steve Gill and Ushani Nanayakkara

Intervention Description (6)--- The team needs to determine well in advance of talking about special education what exactly is the concern (unless there is a clear medical condition impacting the student or high likelihood of an intellectual disability). That is, don't just look at reading; look at the components of reading. Then, create a targeted intervention that will be delivered with pre-testing, progress monitoring, and post-testing (with other students who are like peers with regard to language and educational history). With that you will have growth curves specific to the core issues to compare between students. If this student's growth curve is similar to that of the other students, when given a targeted intervention, then a special education evaluation is likely not the answer. So, place a mark in the matrix based upon the likely impact (e.g., if the interventions haven't been targeted to a specific need then the mark goes more toward the need for more interventions and if the interventions have been targeted, and the results are poor compared to peers, then the mark goes more toward the possible referral).

Expectations in the general education classroom (7)--- All students should be expected to complete assignments, no matter the level of their skills development. So, a student might have lower expectations (only for short periods of time as needed to promote work production), but will still be expected to complete work that is related to the core skills. It is impossible to determine whether or not a student has a specific learning disability if they have not been required to provide output regarding their learning and had the requirements increased with skills development in mind. So, place a mark on the chart based upon the likely impact (e.g., if the student hasn't had consistent expectations of work production then the mark goes toward the need for more intervention and if the student has had consistent work production (not just expectations) and they are performing poorly, then the mark goes more toward the possible referral).

Classroom observation (8)--- If the student has a history of being engaged in the learning process yet is not appearing to learn at the rate of their peers, then that provides data to support a learning difficulty. However, a lack of engagement does not provide any specific data. So, place a mark on the chart based upon the likely impact (e.g., if the student is engaged and making efforts (with poor results) the mark goes more toward the possible referral and any other behavior will likely lead to a neutral mark). For number 8, the matrix is marked from Neutral to Supports a Referral, given that a student who is not doing anything tells us nothing and a student who is trying (yet not succeeding) moves the mark toward Supports a Referral.

Comparison Student Data (9)--- You will place a mark in the matrix based upon the comparison of the growth curves from the data gathered (i.e., if the curve is similar to the other students or indicates better growth (indicating positive learning skills) place the mark in the matrix to indicate a need for further intervention and if the curve indicates a notably slower growth (lack of demonstrated learning) place the mark on the chart to indicate a need for a special education referral. This is about something other than reading, math or writing skills. Specific examples are provided later within this workbook.

Poverty (10)--- If the student is a student in poverty place a mark toward more intervention and if they are not place the mark in neutral. There is a small correlation of poverty to disability, but only because there is a larger correlation of disability to poverty. This item is linked to students in poverty commonly having fewer experiences and exposures that can be related to school preparedness. Also, in some cases, the student's parents are working multiple jobs to ensure basic needs are met, limiting their time/availability to support school expectations. Caution needs to be taken to not correlate poverty to disability, lack of parent care/desire, or lack of positive parent intent. For number 10, the matrix is marked from Supports more intervention to Neutral, given that students in poverty either need more interventions or poverty is not a factor related to disability (meaning a mark in the neutral section).

Behavior (11)--- Is the student demonstrating behaviors that impact their own educational performance? At times, students who are difficult are assumed to be adversely impacting their own education, when there is no documentation to support this assumption. Also, for the purpose of designing interventions, it is important to understand the root cause of the behavior (e.g. is the student having a somewhat reasonable reaction to a very challenging set of life experiences?). If the student is demonstrating behaviors that are adversely impacting their access to their own education, and the behaviors are not a "reasonable" response to a set of challenging life experiences, then the mark is placed toward referral. If the student's behavior is a "reasonable" response to "undesirable" or "unreasonable" life experiences, the mark goes toward more interventions. This is discussed in the examples in following chapters.

Trauma (12)--- Is there evidence that the student has suffered trauma? If there is evidence that the student has suffered trauma, then place a mark toward more interventions. If there is no evidence, place the mark toward neutral. For number 12, the matrix is marked from Supports more Intervention to Neutral, given that students in trauma either need more interventions or trauma is not a factor related to disability (meaning a mark in the neutral section). The impact of trauma can lead to disability if they are not responsive to treatment.

The Parent Interview (13)--- This is meant to be an item in which the totality of the evidence on learning history, parental learning history, sibling learning history, etcetera helps the team to place the mark within the matrix. Also, the team is looking for data that could change the decision toward referral or intervention by itself. This could be an unknown medical condition discovered during an interview, a history of learning difficulties within the family, trauma, or many other possible issues.

Developmental History (14)--- Place a mark on the chart based upon the likely impact after examining developmental milestones, injuries, and/or illnesses (e.g., if there is a history of developmental delay(s) place the mark more toward the possible referral, otherwise place the mark from neutral to more intervention needed).

Each of these 14 concepts are expanded upon in the following chapters.

All Rights reserved by Steve Gill and Ushani Nanayakkara

Analysis Matrix

	1	2	3	4	5	6	7	8	9	10	11	12	13	14
Data supports referral														
Between Neutral and Supports Referral														
Neutral														
Between Neutral and More Interventions														
Data supports more intervention(s)														

After completing the matrix consider the following:

- Are there more marks above or below the Neutral line?

- More marks above Neutral is <u>indicative</u> of the need to make a referral for the possibility of a special education evaluation and more marks below is <u>indicative</u> of needing to design and deliver more targeted interventions.

- Is the difference a large difference? In other words, is it a clear case of choosing either the referral or targeted interventions?

- If not, we recommend defaulting to more targeted interventions. This is based upon the legal requirement that special education services are "need" based services. If the difference is small the results of the data collection are not demonstrating the likelihood of a need.

- It is critical, though, that the teams have these tough discussions and make their decisions based upon their discussions.

All Rights reserved by Steve Gill and Ushani Nanayakkara

Chapter 3: Data Analysis

Do You Know Your School and District Data?

The data regarding proportional or disproportional distribution within special education is something that should be known prior to starting the Matrix Process. A lot of folks really would prefer to get dessert prior to eating their vegetables; however, knowing the data is critical to analyzing how much risk there is in individual student analysis. That is, if you do not know that only 60% of the students in your school, or your district, are successful with the core instruction, you would not know that the student you are examining could be a casualty of a system that is not working for students in general. If you did not know that your district is qualifying Black/African American students as intellectually disabled at twice the rate of the state, you would not know to go the extra mile when evaluating a student who is Black/African American to ensure accuracy. There are many more examples, and your data will tell you where your district has issues. Examining your data helps to ensure that you are not part of creating or maintaining the problem, but instead part of solving the problem.

In order for a school to be able to say a student is not making reasonable progress, they need to know (not think) that their system is working for the vast majority of students and that their work is leading to proportional results. In order to do this, the school (and hopefully the district) needs to analyze their own data.

As a first step, you will need to answer this first set of questions. Later we will provide a list of additional questions that require specific data to help provide answers. Researching the answers to these questions will lead to the systems level and building level analysis needed to understand the nature and location of the problems.

- How do you know that your students as a group are making progress? In order to answer this, you should know the growth rates of your students on the local and state tests as compared to other students in schools in your district, around your state and in the research.

All Rights reserved by Steve Gill and Ushani Nanayakkara

- If you cannot prove average to above-average rates of growth (from the answer to the question above), how do you know the student in question is not actually a curriculum or instruction causality?
- What are the graduation rates of cohorts of students in your district that attended your school, and how do they compare to other groups?
- What are the demographics of the students who are qualified for special education services in your school and district? For example, if 20% of your students receive F/R lunch, do only 20% of your special education students receive F/R lunch?

Once you know the patterns for your school and your district and you have compared them to state and national data, introspection is crucial. If your building (and district) has clear issues with over qualification by race, language learner status, ethnicity, etcetera, how will you be able to factor that into your decision making process?

A question that arises at times is: "What is the difference between ethnicity and race?" As noted within this book, the authors are only using the term race because it is common practice for districts and states to aggregate student data in such a way that disproportionality is represented by race categories. Ethnicity is often related to cultural factors, nationality, and language. Race is a social construct that has a negative history and is primarily based upon the skin color of the individual.

Please note, most schools and districts currently have problems in these areas, so it is critical that staff do not lose hope or become overly critical once these problems are identified. Blame and/or shame do not work in the problem solving process, and actually lead to slow results or no positive results. Instead, staff need to have real and open discussions on why these results are the way they are currently. In education it is profoundly rare to find a staff member who is not a caring and loving individual (even if they try to play it otherwise). We are good people doing hard work. So, take these crucial and difficult conversations seriously, yet focus on solutions and not blame. Once a path toward achieving better results has been set forth, it will take 3-5 years to see large, measurable change.

All Rights reserved by Steve Gill and Ushani Nanayakkara

The following pages contain questions that can lead to further understanding of where the problems are within your school and district. The list of questions cannot cover all the possibilities, especially knowing that new questions can and will arise as data reveals problems. This list provides a starting point, and it is far more extensive than Steve has seen in use in any of the 200+ districts that he has worked with in Washington and other states. The good news is that districts are starting to conduct in depth data analysis (and, luckily, it really is not all that hard).

How to Analyze School and District Data to Help Make Better Decisions

The short answer: easy, get all of the data and start asking and answering questions. The long answer is to start on the surface and keep digging deeper, asking more questions, as the following steps are going to delve into. The following questions and answers are meant to be examples and are not all encompassing. Hopefully this will get teams off to a good start and then their individual circumstances will lead them to ask other questions.

1) What percentage of your district population is qualified for special education services?
2) Break down the results from number 1 by building. Is there any correlation to F/R lunch percentages by building? That is, is your F/R percentage of qualification correlating to your special education qualification rate?
3) How does that compare to the state average? Your first goal is to at least be on the positive side of the state averages, knowing that the state averages might also be demonstrating systems level problems.
4) How does that compare to the national average?
5) How does that compare to districts with strong Response to Intervention (RTI) models in your area?

All Rights reserved by Steve Gill and Ushani Nanayakkara

6) Does your district have a strong RTI Model? In a strong model at least 80% of the students are benefiting from core instruction and your test scores are at or above the state averages.
7) Compare the buildings with strong RTI against the buildings without strong RTI.

The next level of depth:

8) What is the percentage by race and by language spoken for each of the racial groups and each of the language groups within your district?
9) What is the percentage each race and language group is represented within your special education qualified group?
10) Do the numbers appear logical or not? The percentages/proportions should be roughly equal (e.g., 17% of all students are language learners and 17% of the students qualified for special education are language learners, or anywhere between 16-18%).
11) What is the percentage the district uses each of the disability categories (e.g., 37% of the students are qualified using the category of Specific Learning Disability, 12% are qualified using the category of Communication Disorder, etcetera)?
12) How does your district's numbers compare to state and national numbers (found on the state report cards and the OSEP website, respectively)?
13) What are the percentages that these categories are used within each of the racial and linguistic groups?
14) Do the percentages from number 11 match the percentages found in number 12 (i.e., roughly match* and understand that variation in small sample size groups can be meaningless)?

*Given that there will be year-to-year variations and results may be better or worse, yet the trend line must be positively related to the end goal. If there are significant differences, teams need to get together and have real conversations regarding why the differences exist and what the possible solutions are for the disproportionalities. No race, ethnic, nor language group has inherently higher rates of disabilities (qualification rates do not equal disability rates).

15) Does the distribution make sense based upon data? Within a building: Be careful with small data sets.
16) Do the categories of qualification match the percentages at the district level? In other words, if SLD is used 37% of the time across the district, is each building using SLD 37% of the time with their dually qualified students? Is there variation by other groups?
17) Within each building, are there specific problems related to any of the disability categories?
18) Within each building, are there specific problems related to any of the racial groups?
19) Within each building, are there specific problems related to any of the linguistic groups?
20) Within each building, are there specific problems related to children qualified for Free/Reduced lunch?

The first time this is done, for any major "problem area," an individual will need to examine the specific students (likely needing to examine the actual files) and answer the following:

21) What percentage of the students within that group were qualified within the district?
22) Of the students qualified within the district, which buildings were those students qualified in?
23) What was the date of the qualification for ELL students qualified for SLD or SLI? Using this information, what was the student's language acquisition level at that time? Create a chart for this.

It is common that many of the students were qualified for SLD (often SLI, too) while they were at language acquisition level 1 and there is no data to support the problem existed (or exists) in their native language.

Chapter 4: Intervention Focused Examples

You have done the process, and your team has determined more interventions are needed

The following pages will take each of the factors covered by the matrix and provide examples of what might occur as you go through this process as well as examples for possible interventions. Take caution to not to allow these examples to limit your thinking, but instead use them to better understand the intended focus of each item.

The text in red provides the ideas for the item.

Exposure (1)--- The team needs to gather data regarding the exposure the student has had to each of the skill areas that are concerning the team. If the student has not had the same exposure to the skill area as children who have developed the skill to the expected level, then the mark should be made toward more intervention. If the student has had the expected level of exposure, similar to students who have gained the skills, and the student of concern is still not demonstrating the skills, then the mark should be made in the matrix toward referral. The team then can pick between more intervention and referral based upon their interpretation of the data for each skill, weighing exposure against skills gained.

Example for number 1:

The student is a 4-year-old in preschool who is not paying attention to his teacher. The team has determined that the student has not been exposed to an educational setting, nor was the child expected to pay attention to adult instruction. In this case, the team would provide age appropriate instruction (possibly with pictures) to the student. Some of this instruction would focus on learning that when the teacher is talking the students do not talk, need to be facing the teacher, looking at the teacher, and need to be listening to the

All Rights reserved by Steve Gill and Ushani Nanayakkara

teacher with body, eyes and ears. This would then be reinforced with positive comments for appropriate behavior and with a simple behavior chart with stickers. This chart could go home for rewards at home. Then, the parents could review the same instructions with the child, before and after rewarding the student for behaviors that are approximating (then reaching) the expectations.

Experience (2)--- The team, like in number 1, is trying to compare the experiences the student had with the skill of concern against the experiences of a student who is doing well developing the same skill. Exposure is simply contact with something and experience is involvement with the same thing, or direct participation. If the student directly participated in the activities needed to gain the skill(s) at the same level as students who commonly gain the skills, and the student of concern didn't gain the skills, then mark toward referral. If the student of concern did not actively participate in the activities as did the students who gained the skill(s), then mark toward more intervention.

Example for number 2:

This is a student who is in the 4th grade, is a primary Spanish speaker and has had ELL services throughout his schooling. He is making errors in his reading in English that appear language learner based. The team learns that he did not learn to read in Spanish. The team works with the parents to get the OK to help the student learn how to read in Spanish. This required teaching the student the different letter/sound (and blends) correspondence. Then, reading with the student in Spanish and having the student read with his parents in Spanish. Then, working on some of the higher level skills (e.g., using context to understand word meaning). Finally, helping the student understand how the skills transfer from English to Spanish and Spanish to English.

This is a real example. The student had never tried to read in Spanish and had no instruction in Spanish prior to this. This allowed the family to work with their son on reading skills that then transferred to his English reading. The student was highly motivated to read in Spanish and was very successful in a short period of time. He learned the process of reading in English. What was holding back his ability to read in English was English vocabulary, and his Spanish vocabulary was stronger than his English vocabulary.

Expectations (3)--- The team, through observation and interviews, needs to determine the expectations that have been placed upon the student regarding the skill(s) in question. Did the parent(s) or other involved adults expect the student to practice and learn the skill(s) in question? This is not a value judgment. There are times in which the adults, well meaning, will do things for students/children, because it is just easier. Low expectations lead to a mark toward more intervention and high expectations with low results lead to a mark toward referral.

Example for number 3:

In this example the parents of a kindergarten student did not expect him to be able to ride the bus. After arriving at home his mother asked him whether or not he was scared on the bus, and the student began to cry. However, the student's older cousin was on the bus and the teacher had arranged for the student to either sit with his cousin or next to the bus driver.

The student/parent interaction indicated that the student was getting a great deal of attention when he cried if he was asked about the bus ride and he also asked his mother to drive him to and from school. At the same time, the bus driver and the cousin reported that the student was not actually crying on the bus. The older cousin was more than willing to sit with his younger cousin and the bus driver was watching out for the student.

The school helped the parents understand that a kindergarten student showing some fear of riding the bus in September is normal and that all

reports were that their son was not demonstrating any distress until the parents questioned him about the bus ride. The school needed to work with the parent(s) about the words they were using when discussing this. They demonstrated this by discussing the bus ride with the student in front of the parent(s).

Practice (4)--- The team, through observation and interviews, needs to determine the level of practice the student has had with the skill(s) in question. This is again being used to compare the student against students who have developed the skill(s) in question. If the student has not had consistent practice with the skill in question, the mark needs to be placed toward more intervention. If the student has had extensive practice with the skill(s) in question and has not demonstrated success, the mark goes toward referral. Practice needs to be a focused effort on improving a skill, not solely active participation in the skill/activity (e.g., working on phoneme skills development versus pleasure reading).

Example for number 4:

In this case, the student was a second grade girl who had significant meltdowns when another student was "rude" to her. She demonstrated behaviors that were problematic (from name calling to violence) when this occurred. The team spent time with her after a few episodes and did a behavioral mapping process (walking the student through what occurred, when things went "wrong," how the student reacted, and what could be a more appropriate response to get what you want). The student demonstrated that she understood appropriate behavior, but she just "couldn't" do it on the spot and under pressure. Therefore, the team spent the time to practice these difficult situations and the appropriate responses in simulations.

Attendance History (5)--- Any student who has three or more unexcused absences per year or a total of 15 absences per year* or more (excused or not) is outside the norm and is negatively impacted in the learning. So, place a mark in the matrix toward more intervention if they are near or above this level of absenteeism. If the student has had good attendance and is doing poorly, then place the mark in the matrix toward referral.

* This is a yearly rate, so 7-8 absences at midyear, for example, would be outside the norm.

Example for number 5:

In this case, the student is not attending school because they are a language learner who had been very successful in school prior to coming to the United States but who was having a very difficult time here. The team spent some time interviewing the student and she expressed how painful the perceived failures are for her. They discussed how difficult it is at first to be a new English Language Learner and helped her understand the stages that she would be going through and what to expect. Then, the team talked with her about who is her most trusted adult in the school. This individual then set up a schedule of "Check and Connect" times with the student. "Check and Connect" is a system used to assist students with behavior issues and a Google search can lead to information regarding this program.

Intervention Description (6)--- The team needs to determine well in advance of talking about special education what exactly is the concern (unless there is a clear medical condition impacting the student or high likelihood of an intellectual disability). That is, don't just look at reading; look at the components of reading. Then, create a targeted intervention that will be delivered with pre-testing, progress monitoring, and post-testing (with other students who are like peers with regard to language and educational history). With that you will have growth curves specific to the core issues to compare between students. If this student's growth curve is similar to that of the other students, when given a targeted intervention, then a special education evaluation is likely not the answer. So, place a mark in the matrix based upon the likely impact (e.g., if the interventions haven't been targeted to a specific need then the mark goes more toward the need for more interventions and if the interventions have been targeted, and the results are poor compared to peers, then the mark goes more toward the possible referral).

Example for number 6:

The student is within a group of 4 students who have been receiving a targeted intervention on vocabulary skills. The student has been making progress like the other students within this group, so more interventions are needed (see graphs at the end of this chapter). The student sees the success they are having and is motivated. The school not only continues the interventions they are providing, but also helps the student to set-up a self-study program and recruits the parents to participate with a reward system as the student reaches the goals that have been set.

Expectations in the general education classroom (7)--- All students should be expected to complete assignments, no matter the level of their skills development. So, a student might have lower expectations (only for short periods of time as needed to promote work production), but will still be expected to complete work that is related to the core skills. It is impossible to determine whether or not a student has a specific learning disability if they have not been required to provide output regarding their learning and had the requirements increased with skills development in mind. So, place a mark on the chart based upon the likely impact (e.g., if the student hasn't had consistent expectations of work production then the mark goes toward the need for more intervention and if the student has had consistent work production (not just expectations) and they are performing poorly, then the mark goes more toward the possible referral).

Example for number 7:

In this case, the student is a middle school student whose teachers have not created high expectations for the student. First, the school team

(involved teachers and support staff) need to talk about how the research shows that high teacher expectations lead to better results (see John Hattie research). This is something that needs to be believed by all involved. Then, the team needs to agree to expectations that are above the current expectations as a first step (with high expectations as the final goal). This needs to be done in a series of steps, with support for the student to achieve these goals along the way.

Classroom observation (8)--- If the student has a history of being engaged in the learning process yet is not appearing to learn at the rate of their peers, then that provides data to support a learning difficulty. However, a lack of engagement does not provide any specific data. So, place a mark on the chart based upon the likely impact (e.g., if the student is engaged and making efforts (with poor results) the mark goes more toward the possible referral and any other behavior will likely lead to a neutral mark). For number 8, the matrix is marked from Neutral to Supports a Referral, given that a student who is not doing anything tells us nothing and a student who is trying (yet not succeeding) moves the mark toward Supports a Referral.

Example for number 8:

In this example, the team will work with the student to understand why they are not actively participating. Do they not know how to complete the task (lack of skills)? Do they not understand what to do (English skills are not well developed yet)? Or do they do not want to do the work? Once the team understands the core problem, then they need to develop the intervention from this knowledge. For example, if the student does not understand what to do, they can work with the student on self-advocacy skills and have the teacher provide additional checks for understanding.

All Rights reserved by Steve Gill and Ushani Nanayakkara

Comparison Student Data (9)--- You will place a mark in the matrix based upon the comparison of the growth curves from the data gathered (i.e., if the curve is similar to the other students or indicates better growth (indicating positive learning skills) place the mark in the matrix to indicate a need for further intervention and if the curve indicates a notably slower growth (lack of demonstrated learning) place the mark on the chart to indicate a need for a special education referral. This is about something other than reading, math or writing skills. Specific examples are provided within this workbook).

Example for number 9:

The data from the student comparison indicates that the student is learning well in non-core academic areas. In this case, the team can use this data to help the student see him- or herself as a capable learner. They can work with the student to talk about what behaviors they demonstrate in non-academic areas that they might not be demonstrating in the academic areas. In this case, they might feel more successful in the non-academic setting and therefore pay more attention and work harder. The team can encourage the student and reward the same approach during core academic skills areas.

As an example, the PE teacher or Music teacher can rate 5 students from the class in which the student of concern is in, each time that class attends PE or Music. The teacher rates the students during several lessons on how well they learn (if a new lesson) or how well they perform (if an ongoing skill). The teacher should not know who the student of concern is, and should rate all of the students on a 1-5 scale with 1 representing struggling to learn or perform to 5 representing learning quickly or performing at a high level.

Poverty (10)--- If the student is a student in poverty place a mark toward more intervention and if they are not place the mark in neutral. There is a small correlation of poverty to disability, but only because there is a larger correlation of disability to poverty. This item is linked to students in poverty commonly having fewer experiences and exposures that can be related to school preparedness. Also, in some cases, the student's parents are working multiple jobs to ensure basic needs are met, limiting their time/availability to support school expectations. Caution needs to be taken to not correlate poverty to disability, lack of parent care/desire, or lack of positive parent intent. For number 10, the matrix is marked from Supports more intervention to Neutral, given that students in poverty either need more interventions or poverty is not a factor related to disability (meaning a mark in the neutral section).

Example for number 10:

This is an area that is difficult to intervene upon in an individual student manner that is directly related to the poverty itself. However, the impact here is not that poverty creates disability or low skills, but instead how poverty can lead to limited experiences and exposure and how, at times, poverty can adversely impact the amount of time parents are available to provide support. The team in these cases might need to increase the intensity of interventions.

On a related note: One approach that can be taken by a school is to have all staff "adopt" a student who is struggling. In this case all staff means everyone: teachers, custodians, cooks, administration, school psychologists, everyone. In some cases, it might simply be showing attention to the student. Research shows that it only takes one caring adult to help a student. In other cases providing some one-to-one tutoring in a difficult subject may be necessary.

Behavior (11)--- Is the student demonstrating behaviors that impact their own educational performance? At times, students who are difficult are assumed to be adversely impacting their own education, when there is no documentation to support this assumption. Also, for the purpose of designing interventions, it is important to understand the root cause of the behavior (e.g. is the student having a somewhat reasonable reaction to a very challenging set of life experiences?). If the student is demonstrating behaviors that are adversely impacting their access to their own education, and the behaviors are not a "reasonable" response to a set of challenging life experiences, then the mark is placed toward referral. If the student's behavior is a "reasonable" response to "undesirable" or "unreasonable" life experiences, the mark goes toward more interventions.

Example for number 11:

In this example, the student is demonstrating negative behaviors and the staff understands why (the student is reacting to a terrible situation by acting out, but the student does not appear to have a disability). One real case involved a student whose parents were in the middle of a horrible divorce, lived in neighboring cities, had the student one week at a time each, had the student attending school in the different districts depending upon which parent he was with (we didn't know this until much later - this was before computers), and whose little brother was dying of cancer. In this case, the staff needed to work with the student to self-identify when his feelings or thoughts were getting more intense (an antecedent for very bad behavior), then teach the student to ask for a break, and create a safe and comfortable place for the student to take a break.

Trauma (12)--- Is there evidence that the student has suffered trauma? If there is evidence that the student has suffered trauma, then place a mark toward more interventions. If there is no evidence, place the mark toward neutral. For number 12, the matrix is marked from Supports more Intervention to Neutral, given that students in trauma either need more interventions or trauma is not a factor related to disability (meaning a mark in the neutral section). The impact of trauma can lead to disability if they are not responsive to treatment.

Example for number 12:

In this case, it is unlikely that staff members within the school setting have the training to provide the needed therapy, and in many school areas this

type of work is not done within the schools. However, the schools can help to identify what is occurring and encourage the family to seek help. The schools can also help the parents to find resources.

The Parent Interview (13)--- This is meant to be an item in which the totality of the evidence on learning history, parental learning history, sibling learning history, etcetera helps the team to place the mark within the matrix. Also, the team is looking for data that could change the decision toward referral or intervention by itself. This could be an unknown medical condition discovered during an interview, a history of learning difficulties within the family, trauma, or many other possible issues.

Example for number 13:

If the team has chosen to provide more interventions, it is unlikely that significant issues were found within the learning history or family history that an example of intervention in this section would make sense. An example could be a parent(s) letting staff know that they do not have the skills in which to assist their child and the school staff creating a plan in which the student has clear opportunities to get the help they need.

Developmental History (14)--- Place a mark on the chart based upon the likely impact after examining developmental milestones, injuries, and/or illnesses (e.g., if there is a history of developmental delay(s) place the mark more toward the possible referral, otherwise place the mark from neutral to more intervention needed).

Example for number 14:

If the team has chosen to provide more interventions, it is unlikely that significant issues were found within the learning history or family history that an example of intervention in this section would make sense. An example of this could be a student who demonstrated development in expressive and

receptive vocabulary later than expected, and the SLP creating an RTI group in which this student could participate and monitoring the growth of the students throughout the process for student comparison data.

The following 3 graphs represent student growth during intervention or measurement of a specific skill's growth.

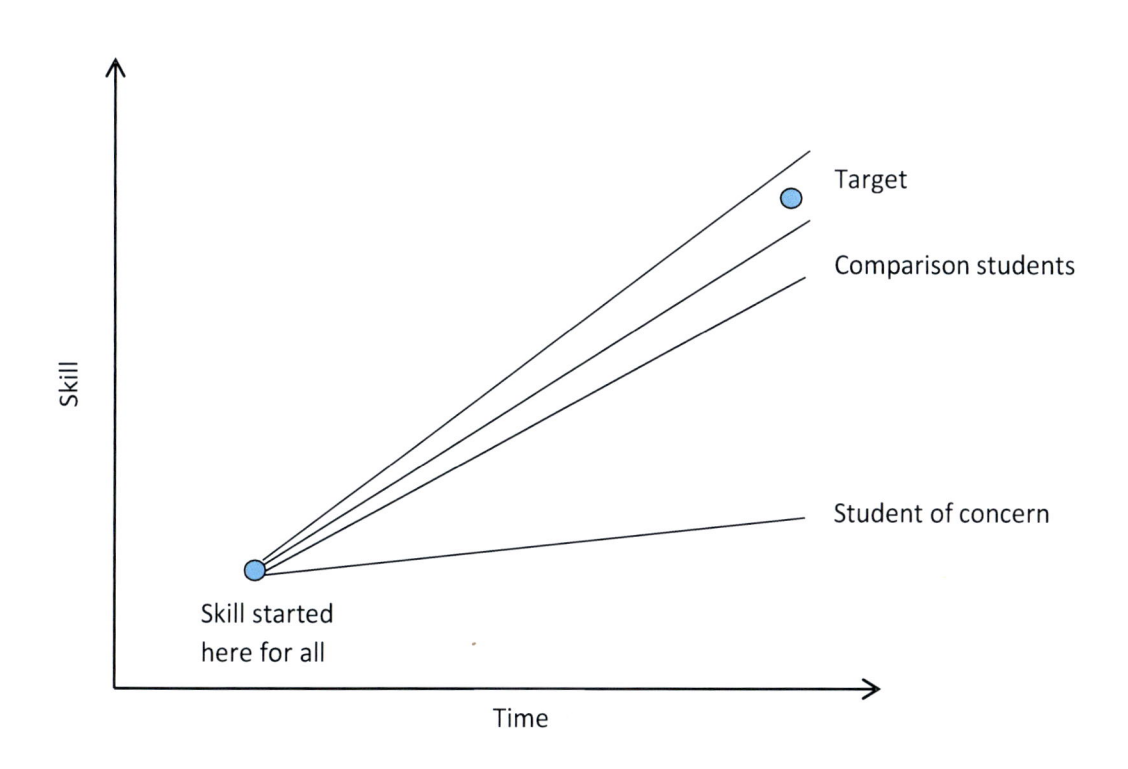

This is a case that represents a student who is showing evidence that is likely to lead to a referral for a special education evaluation. It is critical to never use just one piece of data like this to make critical decisions, but to use this as a portion of the supporting data.

All Rights reserved by Steve Gill and Ushani Nanayakkara

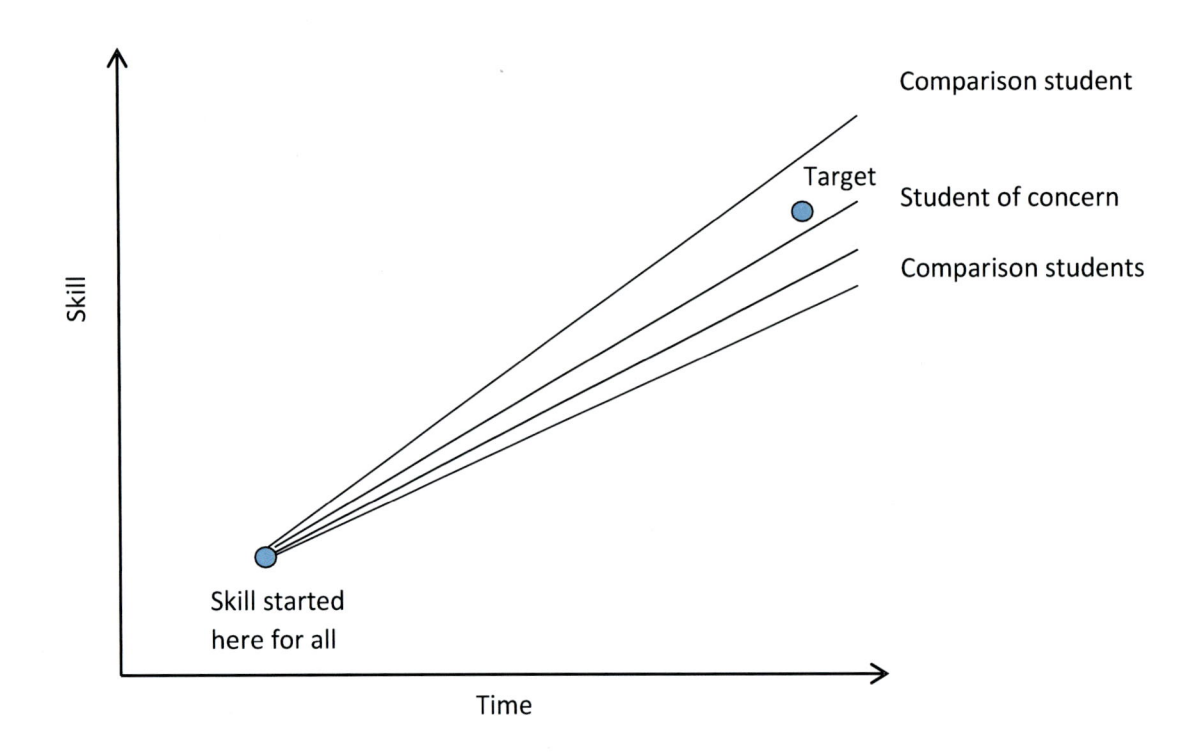

This is a case that represents a student who is showing evidence that is likely to lead to more interventions, given the student is responding well to the intervention. It is critical to never use just one piece of data like this to make critical decisions, but to use this as a portion of the supporting data.

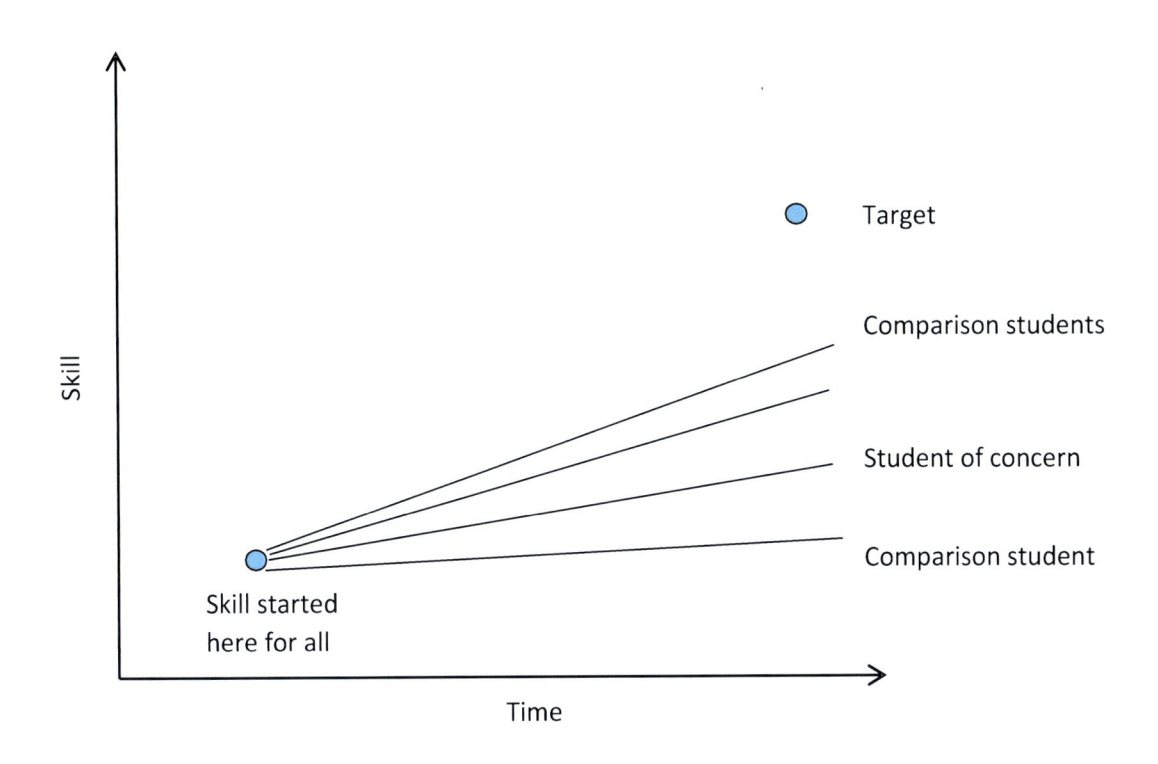

Figure: Graph with Skill on y-axis and Time on x-axis. From a common starting point labeled "Skill started here for all," three lines extend with different slopes to the right: "Comparison students" (steepest), "Student of concern" (middle), and "Comparison student" (shallowest). A separate point labeled "Target" is shown high on the graph.

This is a case that represents, in all likelihood, one of three problems. It is possible that the wrong intervention/materials are being used with the students. It is possible that the person providing the intervention is not a skilled instructor. Or, it is possible that some combination of the first two problems exist. It is critical to never use just one piece of data like this to make critical decisions, but to use this as a portion of the supporting data.

It is very important that during interventions progress is monitored in an ongoing manner. Pre-testing and post-testing can lead to totally erroneous results, given it is possible that the student suffers from distress during the post testing (e.g., parents kept student up while they were arguing about divorce, there is no food in the home, the student is recently homeless, etcetera).

Clay Cook, a leading expert in RTI/MTSS work, while presenting to the Washington State Association of School Psychologists stated that "80% of the time, when intervention fails, the failure is due to a lack of fidelity or the intervention was the wrong intervention." This is critical to remember when analyzing the results of an intervention.

Important: Please remember that the examples we listed in this chapter are to promote thinking with regards to using this process to gather the information needed to create interventions. It is clearly not all inclusive.

Chapter 5: Referral Focused Examples

You Have Your Data and Your Team Believes That a Special Education Referral is the Right Thing to Do

The first step is to analyze the data from the Matrix Process, with the lens of how it applies to whether or not the student should be referred for a special education evaluation, how the data and information applies to that referral, and, if a team is seeking permission to evaluate, how the information can be used during the evaluation process.

The following sections in red are examples of data that is supportive of a referral, and data that might be needed to complete an accurate special education evaluation. These are just examples and are not all inclusive.

Exposure (1)--- The team needs to gather data regarding the exposure the student has had to each of the skill areas that are concerning the team. If the student has not had the same exposure to the skill area as children who have developed the skill to the expected level, then the mark should be made toward more intervention. If the student has had the expected level of exposure, similar to students who have gained the skills, and the student of concern is still not demonstrating the skills, then the mark should be made in the matrix toward referral. The team then can pick between more intervention and referral based upon their interpretation of the data for each skill, weighing exposure against skills gained.

Example for number 1:

In this case, the student has been exposed to the skill of concern. The exposure is similar to that of another student who has developed the skill, yet this student has not developed the skill. For example, a third grade boy who has consistently attended school has been exposed to phonemic awareness skills at all levels in the same manner as other students within your school.

All Rights reserved by Steve Gill and Ushani Nanayakkara

The majority of third grade students in your school have attended your school since kindergarten, as has the student of concern. However, there are only a small number of students with this same skills deficit. This student is one of 10 students who have been participating in a targeted intervention in this area, increasing specific exposure to the skill, and 8 of the 10 are making steady progress toward skills development, yet this student is not. This is evidence supportive of a referral and evidence that can be used during a special education evaluation if that is the decision.

Experience (2)--- The team, like in number 1, is trying to compare the experiences the student had with the skill of concern against the experiences of a student who is doing well developing the same skill. Exposure is simply contact with something and experience is involvement with the same thing, or direct participation. If the student directly participated in the activities needed to gain the skill(s) at the same level as students who commonly gain the skills, and the student of concern didn't gain the skills, then mark toward referral. If the student of concern did not actively participate in the activities as did the students who gained the skill(s), then mark toward more intervention.

Example for number 2:

The example in number one is an example of both exposure and later in experience (direct participation). The targeted intervention and the results (with comparison students) show how the student was directly participating in the skill in question. This is evidence of a student who had similar experience as students who were making progress, yet this student was not. Therefore, it is evidence that is supportive of a referral and could be evidence that can be used during a special education evaluation.

Expectations (3)--- The team, through observation and interviews, needs to determine the expectations that have been placed upon the student regarding the skill(s) in question. Did the parent(s) or other involved adults expect the student to practice and learn the skill(s) in question? This is not a value judgment. There are times in which the adults, well meaning, will do things for students/children, because it is just easier. Low expectations lead to a mark toward more intervention and high expectations with low results lead to a mark toward referral.

Example for number 3:

In this case, the team needs data that supports that the adults (teachers, parents, others) expect the student to achieve/learn the skill(s) in question. This can be a teacher that knows a student is struggling to provide written responses, yet the teacher continues to expect the student to write the best sentences they can write, encourages the student to try in all cases, provides support, and when the student is not doing their best work the teacher holds them accountable to the expectations. And, as the student's skills grow, the expected quality is increased. Then, if these are the expectations and the student is growing at a slower rate than comparison students this can be used as supporting data for a referral and could later be used as support for an accurate special education evaluation.

Number 3 can combine both classroom expectations and parent expectations.

Parent specific example: Think back to the example of the Russian student in chapter 4. In that case, the parents valued learning to read and speak in Russian. The parents did not demonstrate significant concern regarding their child learning English skills. In this case, the student did very little work in English.

Practice (4)--- The team, through observation and interviews, needs to determine the level of practice the student has had with the skill(s) in question. This is again being used to compare the student against students who have developed the skill(s) in question. If the student has not had consistent practice with the skill in question, the mark needs to be placed toward more intervention. If the student has had extensive practice with the skill(s) in question and has not demonstrated success, the mark goes toward referral. Practice needs to be a focused effort on improving a skill, not solely active participation in the skill/activity (e.g., working on phoneme skills development versus pleasure reading).

Example for number 4:

In this case, you could have a student who has always had the expectations to complete work as all other students. The student has consistently completed the expected work, yet the quality is not increasing. Therefore, like other students, they are practicing the skill at the same frequency. Then, the lack of growth in skills is the evidence used to support a referral and could later be used as data to support an accurate evaluation.

Attendance History (5)--- Any student who has three or more unexcused absences per year or a total of 15 absences per year* or more (excused or not) is outside the norm and is negatively impacted in the learning. So, place a mark in the matrix toward more intervention if they are near or above this level of absenteeism. If the student has had good attendance and is doing poorly, then place the mark in the matrix toward referral.

* This is a yearly rate, so 7-8 absences at midyear, for example, would be outside the norm.

Example for number 5:

In this case, you have a student who has very good attendance, yet is doing very poorly in school. Or, you have a student who is not attending because they have a long history of doing so poorly in school and they just find it too painful to attend school. Either of these cases supports a referral and could be evidence used during a special education evaluation.

Intervention Description (6)--- The team needs to determine well in advance of talking about special education what exactly is the concern (unless there is a clear medical condition impacting the student or high likelihood of an intellectual disability). That is, don't just look at reading; look at the components of reading. Then, create a targeted intervention that will be delivered with pre-testing, progress monitoring, and post-testing (with other students who are like peers with regard to language and educational history). With that you will have growth curves specific to the core issues to compare between students. If this student's growth curve is similar to that of the other students, when given a targeted intervention, then a special education evaluation is likely not the answer. So, place a mark in the matrix based upon the likely impact (e.g., if the interventions haven't been targeted to a specific need then the mark goes more toward the need for more interventions and if the interventions have been targeted, and the results are poor compared to peers, then the mark goes more toward the possible referral).

Example for number 6:

In this case, you have had the student in a targeted intervention. This student, when compared to the other students in the same intervention, is making much slower progress or little progress. This is evidence that would support a referral and could be evidence that could be used during a special education evaluation.

Expectations in the general education classroom (7)--- All students should be expected to complete assignments, no matter the level of their skills development. So, a student might have lower expectations (only for short periods of time as needed to promote work production), but will still be expected to complete work that is related to the core skills. It is impossible to determine whether or not a student has a specific learning disability if they have not been required to provide output regarding their learning and had the requirements increased with skills development in mind. So, place a mark on the chart based upon the likely impact (e.g., if the student hasn't had consistent expectations of work production then the mark goes toward the need for more intervention and if the student has had consistent work production (not just expectations) and they are performing poorly, then the mark goes more toward the possible referral).

Example for number 7:

In this case, the team needs data that supports that the adults (teachers, parents, others) expect the student to achieve/learn the skill(s) in question within the classroom setting. This can be a teacher that knows a student is struggling to provide written responses, yet the teacher continues to expect the student to write the best sentences that they can write, encourages the student to try in all cases, provides support, and when the student is not doing their best work the teacher holds them accountable to the expectations. And, as the student's skills grow, the expected quality is increased. Then, if these are the expectations and the student is growing at a slower rate than comparison students this can be used as supporting data for a referral and could later be used as support for an accurate special education evaluation.

Examples 3 and 7 are the same. Number 7 is specific to what is occurring within the classroom regarding work completion. It is the responsibility of the team to discuss how the expectations outside the classroom are both similar and different than those within the classroom. Do those similarities and differences help the team to understand the student? Or do these similarities and differences confuse the student and make the problems worse?

Classroom observation (8)--- If the student has a history of being engaged in the learning process yet is not appearing to learn at the rate of their peers, then that provides data to support a learning difficulty. However, a lack of engagement does not provide any specific data. So, place a mark on the chart based upon the likely impact (e.g., if the student is engaged and making efforts (with poor results) the mark goes more toward the possible referral and any other behavior will likely lead to a neutral mark). For number 8, the matrix is marked from Neutral to Supports a Referral, given that a student who is not doing anything tells us nothing and a student who is trying (yet not succeeding) moves the mark toward Supports a Referral.

Example for number 8:

In this case, you are observing a student who is trying very hard in school, a student who is watching the other students and trying to copy what the other students are doing. Yet this student is having very little success. Or, the student has told an adult(s) that they do not even try the work because it is too difficult for them to complete. Either of these is supportive of a referral. The first example is information that could be useful evidence during a special education evaluation. The second example would need more investigation; given that it could be a valid impression but sometimes is not.

Comparison Student Data (9)--- You will place a mark in the matrix based upon the comparison of the growth curves from the data gathered (i.e., if the curve is similar to the other students or indicates better growth (indicating positive learning skills) place the mark in the matrix to indicate a need for further intervention and if the curve indicates a notably slower growth (lack of demonstrated learning) place the mark on the chart to indicate a need for a special education referral. This is about something other than reading, math or writing skills. Specific examples are provided within this workbook).

Example for number 9:

In this case, you have worked with the PE teacher to rate 4 students in their classroom on a scale of 1 to 5 after each class session. The rating is based upon either how quickly they learned the lesson or how well they performed in relationship to the expectation (not physical skill, but instead doing the steps as defined). Then, a student of concern would likely have the

lowest ratings after 8-10 class session. It is important that the PE teacher does not know who the student of concern is during this process.

Poverty (10)--- If the student is a student in poverty place a mark toward more intervention and if they are not place the mark in neutral. There is a small correlation of poverty to disability, but only because there is a larger correlation of disability to poverty. This item is linked to students in poverty commonly having fewer experiences and exposures that can be related to school preparedness. Also, in some cases, the student's parents are working multiple jobs to ensure basic needs are met, limiting their time/availability to support school expectations. Caution needs to be taken to not correlate poverty to disability, lack of parent care/desire, or lack of positive parent intent. For number 10, the matrix is marked from Supports more intervention to Neutral, given that students in poverty either need more interventions or poverty is not a factor related to disability (meaning a mark in the neutral section).

Example for number 10:

In this case, like noted before, poverty does not create disability. If the team has a student in poverty and the student is known to have had strong exposure and experience with learning activities, yet is still doing poorly in school, then poverty is not a factor that will be related to supporting a special education referral or later an evaluation or qualification. However, if an evaluation is completed on a student who is in poverty, who is known to have had limited exposure, experience, expectations, and/or practice, then the team needs to provide data/reasoning to why the impacts of poverty are not a determining factor in the evaluation decision.

Note: You need to know if your school and district data for poverty predicts referral and qualification rates to determine the size of the problem.

All Rights reserved by Steve Gill and Ushani Nanayakkara

Behavior (11)--- Is the student demonstrating behaviors that impact their own educational performance? At times, students who are difficult are assumed to be adversely impacting their own education, when there is no documentation to support this assumption. Also, for the purpose of designing interventions, it is important to understand the root cause of the behavior (e.g. is the student having a somewhat reasonable reaction to a very challenging set of life experiences?). If the student is demonstrating behaviors that are adversely impacting their access to their own education, and the behaviors are not a "reasonable" response to a set of challenging life experiences, then the mark is placed toward referral. If the student's behavior is a "reasonable" response to "undesirable" or "unreasonable" life experiences, the mark goes toward more interventions.

Example for number 11:

In this example, there is no evidence of life situations that could explain the inappropriate behaviors. Instead, the team might have evidence that the student is behaving poorly due to frustration with their poor academic performance. Or, the student is performing poorly due to behaviors that are interfering with their ability to access their education. Either case is evidence that supports a referral and could be evidence used during a special education evaluation.

Trauma (12)--- Is there evidence that the student has suffered trauma? If there is evidence that the student has suffered trauma, then place a mark toward more interventions. If there is no evidence, place the mark toward neutral. For number 12, the matrix is marked from Supports more Intervention to Neutral, given that students in trauma either need more interventions or trauma is not a factor related to disability (meaning a mark in the neutral section). The impact of trauma can lead to disability if they are not responsive to treatment.

Example for number 12:

In most cases, if the student is a student in trauma, this item cannot be used to support the need for a referral for special education. There could be other factors from other items (e.g., a medical condition) that could be related, yet this item by itself would not be used to support a special education referral in all but the most unusual of circumstances.

The Parent Interview (13)--- This is meant to be an item in which the totality of the evidence on learning history, parental learning history, sibling learning history, etcetera helps the team to place the mark within the matrix. Also, the team is looking for data that could change the decision toward referral or intervention by itself. This could be an unknown medical condition discovered during an interview, a history of learning difficulties within the family, trauma, or many other possible issues.

Example for number 13:

In this case, the team could have found information that the student has a long history of difficulty with multiple learning activities. There could be a history of parental learning difficulties, or there could be a history of siblings with learning difficulties. Any of these could be information used to support a referral or evidence used during a special education evaluation.

Developmental History (14)--- Place a mark on the chart based upon the likely impact after examining developmental milestones, injuries, and/or illnesses (e.g., if there is a history of developmental delay(s) place the mark more toward the possible referral, otherwise place the mark from neutral to more intervention needed).

Example for number 14:

In this case, the team might have found evidence that the student did not meet their developmental milestones on time, or that the student had a significant head injury, or a history of significant learning loss. Any of these could be evidence that is supportive of a referral or could be evidence used during a special education evaluation.

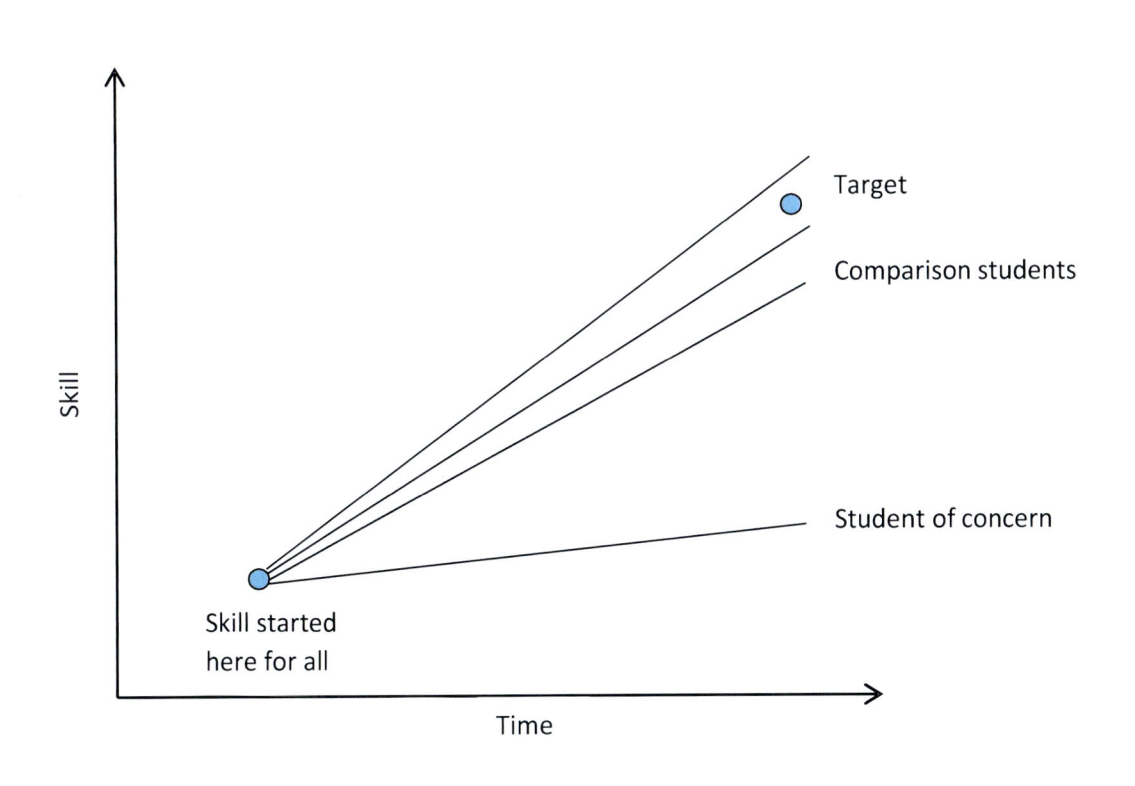

This is a case that represents a student who is showing evidence that is likely to support a referral for a special education evaluation. It is critical to never use just one piece of data like this to make critical decisions, but to use this as a portion of the supporting data.

All Rights reserved by Steve Gill and Ushani Nanayakkara

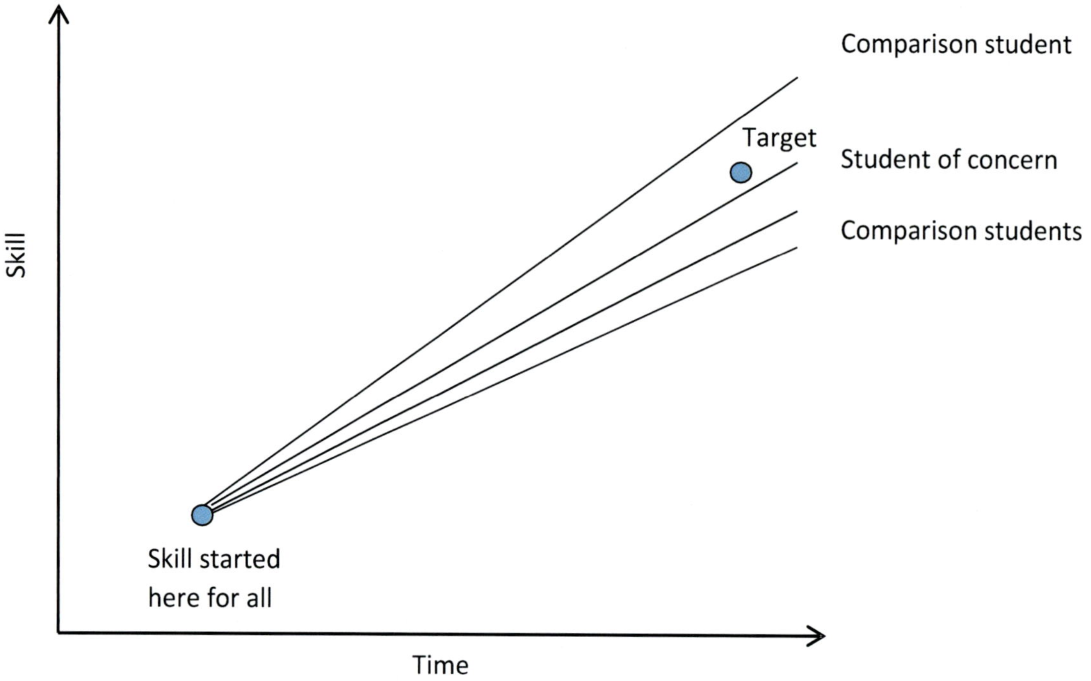
Comparison student
Target
Student of concern
Comparison students
Skill
Skill started
here for all
Time

This is a case that represents a student who is showing evidence that is likely to support to more interventions, given the student is responding well to the intervention. It is critical to never use just one piece of data like this to make critical decisions, but to use this as a portion of the supporting data.

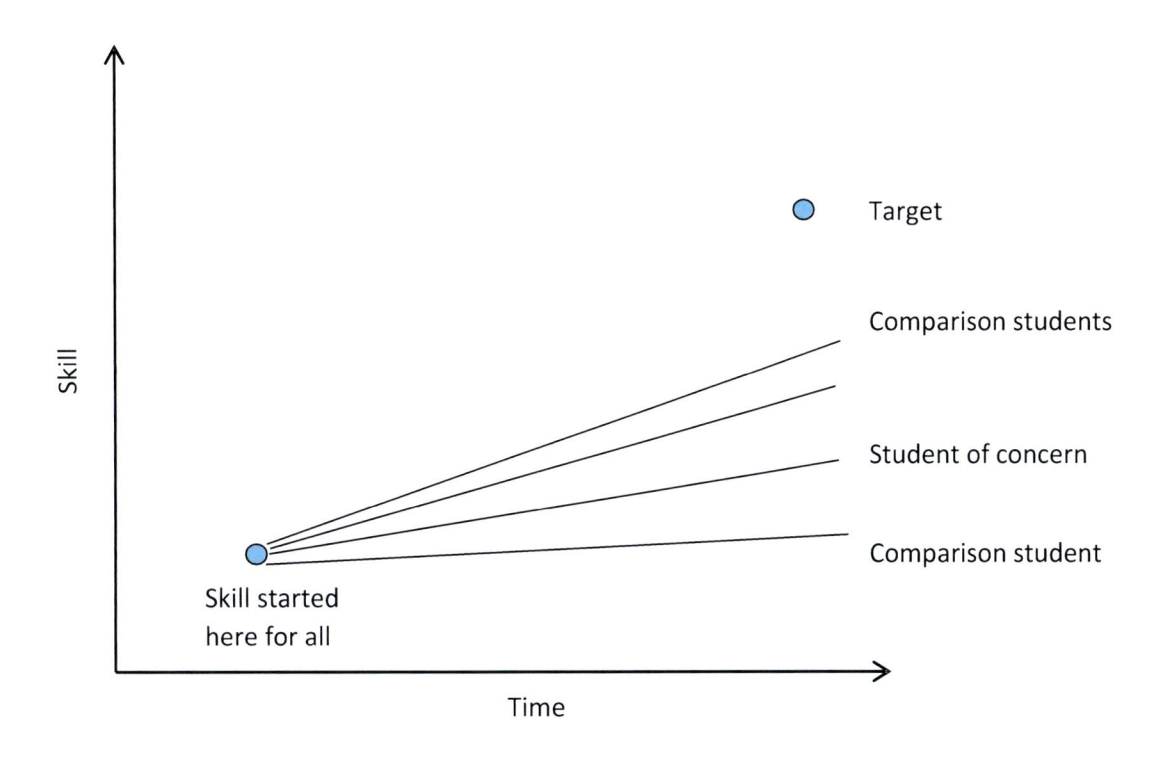

```
    ^
    |
    |                                          O   Target
    |
Skill|                                      _____ Comparison students
    |                                   ___/
    |                               ___/_____ Student of concern
    |                           ___/_____
    |                       O__/_____ Comparison student
    |                    Skill started
    |                    here for all
    +---------------------------------------->
                            Time
```

This is a case that represents, in all likelihood, one of three problems. It is possible that the wrong intervention/materials are being used with the students. It is possible that the person providing the intervention is not a skilled instructor. Or, it is possible that some combination of the first two problems exists. It is critical to never use just one piece of data like this to make critical decisions, but to use this as a portion of the supporting data.

It is critical, during interventions, that progress is monitored in an ongoing manner. Pre-testing and post-testing can lead to totally erroneous results, given it is possible that the student suffers from distress during the post testing (e.g., parents kept student up while they were arguing about divorce, there is no food in the home, the student is recently homeless, etcetera).

Clay Cook, a leading expert in RTI/MTSS work, while presenting to the Washington State Association of School Psychologists stated that "80% of the time, when intervention fails, the failure is due to a lack of fidelity or the intervention was the

All Rights reserved by Steve Gill and Ushani Nanayakkara

wrong intervention." This is critical to remember when analyzing the results of an intervention.

Important: Please remember that the examples we listed in this chapter are to promote thinking with regards to using this process to gather the information needed to create interventions. It is clearly not all inclusive.

Chapter 6: Belief Systems

Our Personal Journey

We are all experiencing our own personal journey, and everyone's journey is unique and different. Learning how to determine whether or not a student needs more interventions, or if a special education referral is more appropriate, is a long learning journey, and one that Steve is still traveling. This journey is made easier or more difficult depending upon each person's willingness and ability to reflect upon their acculturation, their beliefs, their actions (practices) and their results.

We are acculturated from the day we start to understand what is occurring around us. Acculturation is combined with knowledge and this creates belief systems that eventually leads to actions and practices at work. Our practices lead to results, good, bad, or other. We know our results with regards to disproportionality are poor. Our results are not poor because we are actively and knowingly doing bad things (actions or practices), given educators are good and caring people. In order for us to achieve different results, we need to understand what is occurring with our belief systems and acculturation, and how these impact our practices. Then, we can modify our practices and achieve different results. Key questions each person needs to ask themselves, whatever the problem might be, are: "Am I part of creating or maintaining this problem? Or am I part of solving the problem? Our results on disproportionality are very poor, what is my role? Can I possibly know the answer if I don't know the data for my school, district, and state?" Highly unlikely!

One principal that Steve worked with told him, "All of my best teachers are worried about not doing enough and not doing a good enough job and all of my weakest teachers believe they have nothing to learn and are working harder than everyone else." We (the authors) believe that when there is a situation at work (or in life) in which things do not go right or do not go well, the very first thoughts should be about the following: What could I have done differently? What could I have done better? What can I learn from this? This mindset is likely to lead to learning from our mistakes and remaining a learner throughout our career (and life for that matter).

All Rights reserved by Steve Gill and Ushani Nanayakkara

Therefore, each of us needs to examine our belief systems and our acculturation, in order to help us understand if we either help to create some of the disproportionality or if we are part of maintaining existing disproportionality. This process is difficult and at times painful. However, it is necessary for us to figure out how we can be part of the solution, a goal each and every one of us should strive to achieve.

The following pages are meant to provoke thinking and to provide you with examples to help stimulate others' thinking. Hopefully this will also evoke emotions, as emotions help us to remember what we have learned. For example: a parent may try to teach their 3-4-year-old a new word that isn't important to the child, and the child just does not learn the new word. But when the parent gets cut off by another driver and responds, "$ *&^ @#$ $#@#", the child only having heard this phrase once, uses it the following day in correct context, with correct intonation, and with emotion.

So, as you read this, think about:

Acculturation → Belief Systems → Practices → Results

Think about whether you are a part of creating, maintaining, or fixing the problems in your system, and what evidence you have to support your view of where you stand in your system. We are good and caring people, we can use the emotions to fuel a desire to learn more, change our practices, and support others to change their practices.

The reason for this is that our results occur not by chance, but as a result of our practices. Our practices occur based upon what we believe in and our belief systems are a combination of our knowledge and our acculturation.

How we are acculturated creates a lens through which we see the world. The three stories in the following pages provide examples of this.

The information that follows is provided to build knowledge and hopefully encourage individuals to continuously monitor and challenge personal beliefs and practices.

All Rights reserved by Steve Gill and Ushani Nanayakkara

Chapter Layout:

1) **We See What We Are Acculturated To See:** Real world examples of acculturation creating a lens.
2) **Steve's Personal Educator Journey:** Real world example of developing over time, making mistakes, gaining new knowledge, learning, changing practices.
3) **Steve Hirsh's and Walter Gilliam's Research:** Research that shows the impact of our biases.
4) **Monolingual Nation:** Real world examples that help us see what could be unrealistic expectations and/or a lack of reasonable expectations.
5) **Literacy and Intelligence:** Knowledge to help us see things differently.
6) **Poverty:** Research that show our results, and indicates biases.
7) **Qualification Versus Disability:** Research that shows that our results do not follow logical patterns, nor our "spoken" beliefs.
8) **Reading and Referrals:** Research that indicates our system, results and beliefs have significant flaws.
9) **Race versus Disability:** Research that shows our results, again, do not follow logical patterns, nor our "spoken" beliefs

1. We See What We Are Acculturated To See

The following three examples are meant to help you understand that we see what we are acculturated to see. Our acculturation provides a lens which we look through and that changes our view of the world.

Ushani is one of the few people on earth who is a German/Sri Lankan. Sri Lanka is an island in the Indian Ocean, just south of India. Therefore it's easy to assume that Germans and Sri Lankans do not commonly meet one another in such a way that relationships are likely to begin. Additionally, of the Germans and Sri Lankans who do meet, not all of them speak a common language. Then, of the Germans and Sri

Lankans who do meet and who do speak a common language, not very many are likely to form a romantic relationship, get married, and have children.

People who meet Ushani struggle greatly in figuring out her heritage and make many assumptions. Ushani has had numerous experiences in which someone has spoken Spanish to her, assuming that she is a Latina, only to have Steve respond. This tends to leave the person completely dumbfounded. They probably wonder why the Latina* doesn't speak Spanish, but the older white guy does (some folks have literally told Steve that it is confusing to them to have an older white guy speaking Spanish with them). When Ushani is around people who are Black or African American, she is often thought to be a light skinned Black or African American woman. Then, there are times in which people believe that Ushani is a woman from India (to her Sri Lankan relatives, this is totally illogical). Virtually no one guesses that Ushani is from Sri Lanka. This is in large part because people rarely have a mental picture of what someone from Sri Lanka looks like (a lack of knowledge, a lack of this being part of one's acculturation). Did you have a picture of what someone from Sri Lanka might look like prior to this? Nobody ever guesses German, and many Germans have struggled to "see" Ushani as a German. Some Germans think she is Turkish; others think she is black. A friend of the family once asked her mother, "Don't you think it will be difficult for a black child to grow up in Germany?" when Ushani's mother considered moving back to Germany.

People are not acculturated to imagine someone who looks like Ushani as German. Acculturation created lenses for each of these groups that impacted their decision making and their actions, like it does for all of us.

*Steve usually uses the terms Latino(a) and black, instead of Hispanic and African-American, given his acculturation. This is an important point about cultural competence versus cultural responsiveness that we will discuss near the end of this chapter.

The following example from Steve's experience as a child with an extreme speech impediment and aphasia illustrates how acculturation and belief systems can create lenses through which people interpret the world. Steve's grandmother told him the following story many times. When Steve was 3 to 4 years old, Steve's parents were convinced by their friends that he must be "retarded," the term of the time. Eventually, his parents took him to Seattle Children's Hospital for an evaluation. The first person who saw Steve was a Speech and Language Pathologist, and this person told Steve's parents that not only was he not "retarded," he might actually be bright. That same afternoon Steve was evaluated by either Nancy or Hal Robinson (The Robinson Center on the University of Washington Campus) and Steve's parents were told he was gifted. A strange day in the life of a child who had no idea what was going on. The jury is still out regarding who was right (that is meant of be funny ☺).

During the time Steve's parents were convinced by others that he might be "retarded," at an age of 3-4 years old, Steve was reading and playing chess with adults. Most folks were sure Steve was just looking at the books and they didn't believe his mother's claim that he was reading (given nobody could understand what he was saying). The chess was pretty hard to deny, since people could see it occur. So, what is the point of this story? As a child Steve could not effectively communicate and was therefore seen by others to be cognitively limited, or "dumb." In our society, people who don't speak English are often seen as unlikely to be intelligent*. However, in our schools with lots of language learners, it is possible that the smartest child in the school does not yet speak English.

*Steve has noticed during his training events that people in the audience who speak English as a second or later language all nod their heads in agreement when this point is made.

Have you ever seen an interview with Tiger Woods in which he talks about how much it bothers him that he is virtually never seen as an Asian man? Do you ever think of Tiger Woods as an Asian man? Or, just as a Black or African American man? Tiger Woods expresses how he sees this as disrespectful to his mother and the heritage he has inherited from her.

There are many other examples in our world, yet this provides a window into how acculturation creates a lens through which we view our world. We need to examine ourselves to see how our acculturation is creating our lens.

All Rights reserved by Steve Gill and Ushani Nanayakkara

2. Steve's Personal Educator Journey: The painful life lessons

When Steve was in graduate school there was no coursework on the assessment of language learners; it was not even discussed. Steve began his career in the Tacoma School District and he quickly realized that he lacked skills in the area of evaluating language learners. Then he learned that finding information on this topic was next to impossible.

The first event to shape Steve's experience was a little boy who walked into his office with a doctor's script that said "ADHD, qualifies for special education as a student with an Other Health Impairment." School psychologists often do not take this any better than medical doctors would take school psychologists making medical diagnosis and sending the families to the doctor's office. Steve called the doctor and asked him how he made the diagnosis, and the doctor responded, "I was educated at Harvard." After hearing this a few times Steve expressed his lack of care regarding the doctor's education. The doctor finally said, "I interviewed the family." Steve responded, "You speak Vietnamese?" The doctor then told Steve to do things that would be anatomically difficult to achieve, Steve responded, and eventually the doctor hung up the phone (it is likely Steve was having a better time than the doctor). It was later discovered that this student did not have ADHD and the family had no idea what had occurred with this.

Steve moved on with his career, eventually landing in a district that had a large percentage of Spanish speaking students in special education. Steve decided that he wanted to be bilingual and bi-literate, so he started taking night classes. After a year, he might have achieved the ability to ask where the bathroom is or order a beer, but not much more. With a great deal of luck, Steve ended up eating dinner with Dr. Stephen Krashen, one of the leading experts in the world on language acquisition. Dr. Krashen told Steve what he needed to do, and it was all about comprehensible input. So, Steve started to read books in Spanish, starting with kindergarten level books, until he mastered those, then first grade level books, and when he mastered those, second grade level books (reading The Mouse and the Motorcycle with great excitement), and so on. Steve eventually had a dilemma. The only books at his level that he could find were the Twilight series, something rather hard on his ego (please note, this story is going somewhere). Steve thought he was safe reading this at school, and was walking to the staff lounge holding this book when a nice little girl that Steve knew well asked him if she could borrow the book after he was done with it. Steve first thought "Why?" believing she could not read the book because she was qualified for special education for reading, had never lived in a Spanish speaking country, and had no formal education in Spanish. Steve told her, "I will buy you brand new copies of the books if you stop by my office each week to, 1) Tell me about what you read, 2) Tell me about what you liked, 3) Tell me about what you think will happen next." This did not go as Steve thought it would go. Not only did she read every one of these books, she provided Steve replies to his questions ad nauseam. The point to this story is that not only was she qualified for special education for reading in English, not only had she never been formally educated in Spanish, not only was she reading at a higher level in Spanish than in English, Steve was the school psychologist who had qualified her for special education. This was a painful learning moment for Steve. A moment that required a lot of reflection.

Soon after this Steve began working for the Kent School District as the ESA Coach (the coach for all of the school psychologists, speech and language pathologists, occupational therapists, and physical therapists). He was offered the opportunity to start the district supported ELL graduate level program through Heritage University. This is where the work on the ELL Critical Process began, and the puzzle pieces started coming together.

The point of these stories is that each of us is on a journey of skills development. This can only occur if each of us is honest with ourselves about our mistakes, honest with ourselves regarding the impact of our acculturation, honest with ourselves about our skills (or lack of skills), honest with ourselves about our knowledge (or lack of knowledge) and if we do something to work on our own issues (Yoda said, "There is no try, there is do and not do"). We also need to be willing to examine our own issues around belief systems and race, in order to improve and focus on making a difference in disproportionality.

All Rights reserved by Steve Gill and Ushani Nanayakkara

3. Steve Hirsch's Research

Steve Hirsch is a school psychologist in Washington State who has been a leader within the state school psychologist association for many years. Dr. Hirsch completed the following research as part of other ongoing projects and presented the information at the state school psychologist conference, trying to help people understand that we have biases that we are not aware of, and that those biases are impacting our work. The slides below represent the results after staff were given identical data on four students, in which the only difference was the name of the student and the country of origin.

The first slide below shows that, with identical data, the Latino students were significantly more likely to be referred for special education evaluations. The second slide below, with identical data for each of the students, shows that there are significantly different rates of recommendation to exit student from special education, based solely upon their race.

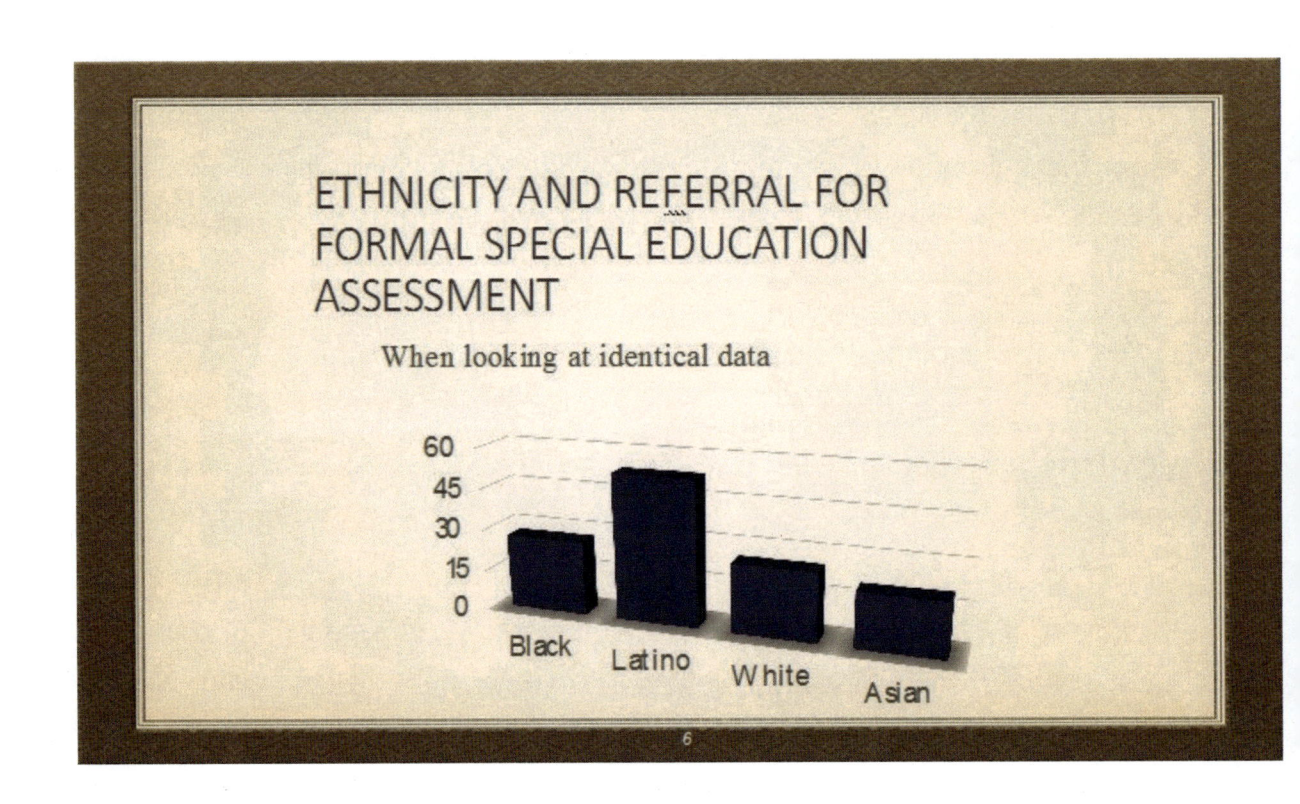

ETHNICITY AND REFERRAL FOR FORMAL SPECIAL EDUCATION ASSESSMENT

When looking at identical data

[Bar chart showing values for Black (~25), Latino (~55), White (~15), Asian (~10)]

All Rights reserved by Steve Gill and Ushani Nanayakkara

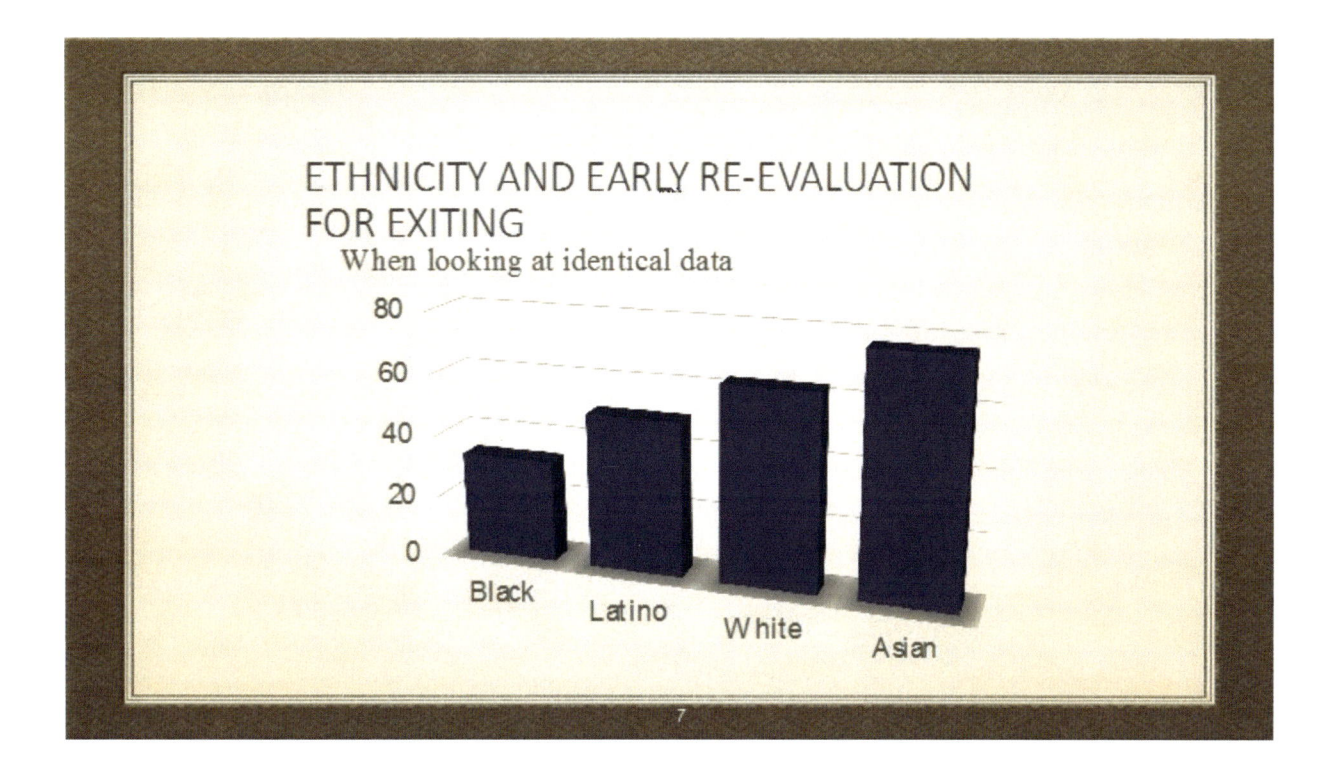

ETHNICITY AND EARLY RE-EVALUATION FOR EXITING
When looking at identical data

[Bar chart showing values for Black (~30), Latino (~45), White (~55), Asian (~65)]

We all want to believe that we do not have biases, yet we all have them. It is a natural part of being human. We need to have the courage to examine our biases and the impact of those upon our work.

Another excellent example of research on biases is the research completed at Yale University by lead researcher Walter Gilliam. This research had a group of teachers watching videos of children playing, and they were asked to identify the challenging behaviors as they saw them occur in the videos. There were four children, one white boy, one white girl, one black boy, and one black girl. The researchers used eye scanning technology to watch the eyes of the teachers. The teachers watched the black boys significantly more than the other children. The interesting part is that there was no challenging behavior at all occurring in the videos. The research has other very important components and is well worth reading. As noted earlier in this book, black boys are identified as behaviorally disabled at a much higher rate than other children. What if that is a result of school staff expecting them to behave poorly, watching them more closely than other children, and reacting differently given those expectations? Is it also possible that these children behave differently because they feel that they are being treated unfairly, singled out?

4. Monolingual Nation: Our Expectations of Our Students

Are we really the "monolingual" nation???

Are our expectations of our students based upon a knowledge of the challenges that they face? And, do we have any personal experience related to the depth of those challenges? We have created the following food for thought. However, a small joke before beginning: What do you call someone who speaks 3 or more languages? Multilingual. What do you call someone who speaks 2 languages? Bilingual. What do you call someone who speaks just one language? American…. ☺

Steve was studying in Valencia, Spain, in a large language school. There were over 100 students, mostly from Northern Europe. There were only 2 Americans, and both Americans were receiving a LARGE quantity of negativity regarding Americans and Americans' ethnocentricity. "You people don't even care enough to learn another language." After about a week of this, Steve responded (in a nice way) that he had had enough. Eventually after more commentary, Steve pointed out that they used their best English speakers/writers to create signs in English and every single one of the signs had an error. They originally thought this was impossible. Steve, at their urging, took them around the building to every sign with English text and explained the errors (all the signs had errors). This eventually became a game, with all the students who were attempting to learn English taking Steve around the campus to talk about every sign they could find.

In Sri Lanka, in the big city of Colombo, it is not difficult to find someone who speaks English (it is very common throughout the schools to teach English). During one of their trips Steve and Ushani stayed in a hotel outside of Colombo. The hotel stated that it would always have someone available who spoke English. One day Steve and Ushani needed some towels, and went to the front desk. The front desk sent for the person who could speak English. Steve and Ushani then worked with this person for quite some time trying to express what they needed (this could have been a Saturday Night Live skit, or a Candid Camera scene).

After visiting Sri Lanka, Steve and Ushani visited Ushani's family in Germany. After a few days, Steve told Ushani she didn't need to interpret any longer for him, he was content to just smile and nod his head. Have you ever noticed a language learner looking at you, smiling and nodding their head? Have you ever done this with your spouse, significant other, or a good friend when you didn't understand the topic that they kept talking about? Do you know what that means? It means they (or you) got tired of concentrating and trying to make sense of what the others were saying and chose to just nod and smile.

The point to this story is not to pick on any other group, but to challenge the idea that everyone else speaks multiple languages, that everyone speaks English, that speaking a little bit of another language is being bilingual or multilingual. The point is that we are not just expecting our English Language Learners to know something about their store or business, we are not expecting them to hold simple conversations. Instead, we are expecting them to function on high stakes tests. And, if they do not function well on these tests we wonder whether or not they have a disability....

Camino de Santiago

ATENCIÓN CICLISTAS
PENDIENTES FUERTES EN 15 Km
CIRCULE CON PRECAUCIÓN

ATTENTION CYCLISTS
OUTSTANDING STRONG IN 15 Km
CIRCULATE WITH CAUTION

All Rights reserved by Steve Gill and Ushani Nanayakkara

The sign in Spanish and English is an example of the type of sign seen in Spain. It is highly unlikely that anyone who speaks only English would understand what they are facing along this path. The English should say:

Attention Cyclists

Steep Hills in/for 15 kilometers

Ride with caution.

Without actually being on the path it is impossible to know if the sign is meant to say "in" 15 kilometers or "for" 15 kilometers.

5. Literacy and Intelligence

A belief held here in the United States is that people who cannot read are on average of lower intelligence. There could be some correlation in countries with exceptionally high rates of literacy. However, some knowledge is needed to reduce the overgeneralization of this belief. There are roughly 7,000 languages on earth and about 100 years ago only an estimated 2,000 of these languages had a written system. Some of the remaining 5,000 languages had written forms, but only very few people knew them. Over the last 100 years, people from these 5,000 or so languages have in many cases worked very hard to create a written form for their language, fearing that the language would be "lost" if it did not have a known, documented and used written form. Some of these languages have only had a written form for roughly 50 years.

The Kent School District is in King County (along with Seattle). Within King County there is a very large Somali population. What we have read about the Somali language indicates that there were 5-6 written forms for Somali that were not widely known or widely used. Then, in the late 1960's a new written form was agreed upon. Given how young this written form is, the literacy rate in Somali is currently estimated at under 30%. There are many languages that are in this same place right now. Therefore, in situations like this, a lack of reading skill is more likely related to a lack of exposure, experience, expectation and practice. And, in situations like this, a lack of reading skills is not likely to be related to intelligence.

6. Poverty

When working with large groups of educators and asking the following question, rarely is there someone who is willing to raise their hand and say "yes":

Do people in poverty have higher rates of disabilities?

The answer is yes, but not based upon what some people might be thinking. The answer is yes because people with disabilities have higher rates of poverty. Reading deficits exist with roughly 80% of all students in special education. In our country, someone who cannot read, on average, is going to have a much more difficult time obtaining a living wage job. Therefore, there is some causation from disability to poverty, and a small correlation of poverty to higher rates of disability. Sadly, though, the research shows that students in poverty are frequently over identified for special education even though the correlations/causations noted above are about their parents and not about them. And, poverty does not cause disabilities, but instead can be linked to less exposure and experience, and sometimes less time for parent support. These factors do not make a student disabled, but instead create a situation in which a student is likely to have a more difficult time in school. The following pages document some research Steve completed in Washington State, showing that our qualification rates and our poverty rates are linked, sadly.

The following quote from the University of Texas at Austin is included to provide additional insight into this issue.

Education and Transition to Adulthood, Information on Learning Disabilities, available at: http://www.utexas.edu/cola/etag/Related%20Sites/Learning-Disabilities.php

Although the research focus has primarily been on the disproportionate labeling of racial minorities with LD, the research team found that differences in the rates of being labeled are more dramatic

All Rights reserved by Steve Gill and Ushani Nanayakkara

by socioeconomic status (SES) than by race. The odds of being labeled with LD are much higher among low SES than high SES high school students, regardless of whether the student is black or white. In fact, low SES white high school students are as likely as low SES black or Hispanic high school students to be labeled with LD, but much greater proportions of racial minorities are in that high-risk low SES group.

In contrast to black and white high school students, high SES Hispanic high school students are as likely as low SES Hispanic high school students to be labeled with LD. The team found that disproportionate labeling of Hispanic students with learning disabilities in high school is attributable to the over-labeling of language minorities.

The team also found that students attending higher poverty schools are actually less likely to be labeled with LD, and that systematic differences in academic achievement by SES, race, and linguistic status are a major factor in disproportionality.

7. Qualification vs Disability

Special Education Qualification Rates in Washington State and the Link to Free and Reduced Lunch Rates

In 2014 Steve checked the data for 295 school districts. No district was purposely left out of the data, with the exception of school districts in the data set that are not actually comprehensive school districts (e.g., School for the Blind). Therefore, with a set of 250 districts, it is highly unlikely that any district missed would impact the noted trends.

For 16 districts the special education qualification percentages fell below 10% of the total student population. For 15 of the 16 school districts (the 16th noted separately below), the average student population in the districts was 145 students. The number 145 is the total student population and not just total for the special education population.

There were 32 districts with special education qualification percentages above 18% of the total student population. The average student population across these districts was 392 students. As above, 392 represents the total student population and not just the special education population.

In the State of Washington, 45.9% of the students are on Free or Reduced Lunch. The average percentage of F/R Lunch for the districts below 10% special education qualification rate was 24%. The average percentage of F/R Lunch for the districts above 18% was 75.6%.

The only medium/large district with a percentage below 10% of the student population qualified for special education services was the Issaquah School District, at 8.8%. It is interesting to note that the Issaquah School District has some of the highest state test scores noted during this research.

Although the F/R Lunch difference is extreme, there is no way to prove that it is a causal factor. Yet, many research studies have indicated that poverty is a very high predictor of special education qualification. This occurs even though it would be very hard to argue, beyond a minimal percentage difference, that poverty has any correlation to rates of disabilities, and no causal relationship.

It is interesting to note that virtually all of the districts on the extremes of the range have very small student populations. In all of these cases, one or only a few people are making the qualification decisions.

We have a lot of power in influencing outcomes, and, hopefully a lot to think about in our daily work for positive student outcomes.

It would be hard to examine this data and not see the human impact. These points are being repeated throughout the book given that "we" have a very hard time seeing ourselves involved in any of the negative results (we being that universal we). However, most staff have not examined the data in their schools and district. We need to have the courage to look closely at our work and to begin to solve problems as they appear. The data is not the way it is because so few people are involved in the problem. Wherever there is a problem, a lot of staff members were involved in creating the problem (remember, not bad people, just bad results). This could seem to contradict what was said above. However, in the problem noted above just a few people had "control" over the outcome, yet many people had input and involvement. So, the big "we" could have stopped the problem if "we" recognized the problem. We need as many or more people involved in the solutions.

The research has shown that the category of specific learning disability, the largest of the categories and the category most frequently disproportional, is heavily impacted by human error, judgment, and/or bias.

8. Reading and Referrals
Qualification rates are not equivalent to disability rates

Schools and systems using RTI or MTSS with fidelity have higher test scores and lower rates of disability qualification. We are using this as evidence of over qualification, along with Carnine's research and the SLD research. This information, like some of the other information, is repeated. The hope is that looking at things from different angles might create new meaning and knowledge for the reader.

Specific Learning Disability is a category that was, more or less, created for the special education world. It is the only category that greatly increased beyond population change from 1975 to 2004, when the special education population in the United States peaked between 2000 and 2004, and has since been dropping. It is the main category to decrease in size since 2004. The SLD category tripled in numbers from 1975 to 2004, eventually being the category in which roughly 50% of all special education students were qualified. Interestingly enough, the decrease in this category started with the federal law that included the usage of RTI qualification. It is easy to see the decrease in the SLD category aligning with the increased usage of RTI within the school systems. At last check, SLD now represents roughly 39.2% of all students qualified for special education. (This was written in 2016 looking at the most current OSEP published data).

The following quotes provide a lot to think about and are followed by ways to mitigate these concerns.

All Rights reserved by Steve Gill and Ushani Nanayakkara

Dr. Carnine (University of Oregon) testifying to the Senate

- "Moving to a response to intervention model can dramatically reduce the long-term failure that is often associated with the IQ-achievement discrepancy formula. 70 to 90 percent of the most at risk children in Kindergarten through 2nd grade can be brought to the average range with effective instruction."

The research into well-implemented RTI or Tiered Intervention has shown that many students who would have previously qualified under SLD have been appropriately served (and have better long term outcomes) through interventions implemented within the general education setting.

Dr. Torgeson from Florida

- "Within 1 year following the intervention, 40% of the children were found to be no longer in need of special education services."
- This was only 8 weeks of intervention at 2 hours per day and the children were labeled "with severe reading disabilities…"

Whether looking at this research or the research on the Lindamood Bell approach, it is easy to see that short-term intensive intervention that is focused on the specific needs of the children shows us that many children do not have disabilities, but instead are casualties of our system. The research noted above was with children considered to have "severe reading disabilities." Studies show that similar methods with students who would be considered to have mild reading disabilities have results of up to 80% of students no longer needing special education services.. Think about the implications. What if 50% of all students in special education (taking the 80% of SLD students and adding a small error rate in the other categories that are "soft") do not actually have disabilities and actually just need intensive interventions?

Is this really happening???

All Rights reserved by Steve Gill and Ushani Nanayakkara

A snapshot of one district's data.... Percentage ELL qualified for special education by building

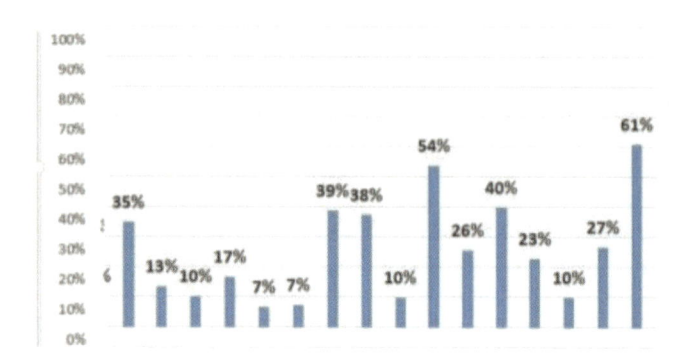

[Bar chart showing percentages by building: 35%, 13%, 10%, 17%, 7%, 7%, 39%, 38%, 10%, 54%, 26%, 40%, 23%, 10%, 27%, 61%]

ALL RIGHTS RESERVED BY STEVE GILL

The graph above is from one of the school districts that Steve worked with on ELL and Special Education Issues. However, Steve has seen this same type of data across numerous districts, and for both ELL and non-ELL students. Some of this is caused by small data sets and how they can provide results that are more random than real. However, this type of pattern is common enough that the problem is beyond small sample size issues. Even after subtracting out small sample problems, this type of graph shows that whether or not a student qualifies for special education can change depending upon the school they are in at the time. This is more information to show staff that qualification rates do not equal disability rates.

What if students are not getting their needs met?

All Rights reserved by Steve Gill and Ushani Nanayakkara

RTI and ELLs

ELL students in schools that do not have an "RTI" model in place are 3 times as likely to be identified for special education.

Source --- Rhodes, Ochoa, Ortiz

Intervention versus Qualification for Special Education....

The quote above from Rhodes, Ochoa and Ortiz is very similar to the data from districts Steve has worked with.

The districts that do not provide targeted interventions in a systematic manner frequently have 2 to 3 times as many ELL students qualified for special education services (when compared to non-ELL students). Given that special education qualification rates across the nation are in the 12-13% range, ask yourself whether or not you believe that it is possible for 24-39% (a range from 2 x 12% to 3 x 13%) of any group could possibly all be disabled? Is your district one of these districts? Are you part of maintaining, creating or solving the problem? In contrast, there are schools who have high rates of success on state and national testing and they frequently have much lower rates of special education qualification. In the Kent School District, the three highest performing schools at the time of writing this book had special education qualification rates of 2.5%, 4%, and 5%.

Good People, Caring People, Poor Results

All Rights reserved by Steve Gill and Ushani Nanayakkara

Education Week on Disproportionality

"... African-American students were nearly or greater than twice as likely as white students to be classified with emotional or intellectual disabilities

In other words, there are kids who are placed in these programs because educators either don't want to deal with them, don't know how to deal with them, or don't know how to be responsive to them.

Scholars generally don't blame racial disproportionality in special education on outright discrimination. Instead, they say it typically derives from systemic flaws within a school or district's instructional culture that allow for some disadvantaged students to fall through the cracks."

Keeping Special Ed in Proportion, by Anthony Rebora, available at: http://www.edweek.org/tsb/articles/2011/10/13/01disproportion.h05.html

ALL RIGHTS RESERVED BY STEVE GILL

Our problems are not about bad people doing bad things, given educators are good and caring people doing their best. The poor results as noted in the quote above and the following quote are about systems level flaws that usually can be traced back to unconscious bias (our acculturation and our belief systems) and a lack of knowledge (what to do differently).

Report to Congress on Disproportionality

Using data from the U.S. Department of Education, analyses suggest that Black children are 2.88 times more likely than White children to be labeled as having mental retardation and 1.92 times more likely to be labeled as having an emotional/behavioral disorder (Losen & Orfield, 2002). Research suggests that unconscious racial bias, stereotypes, inequitable implementation of discipline policies, and practices that are not culturally responsive may contribute to the observed patterns of identification and placement for many minority students."

Information from the *Twenty-fourth Annual Report to Congress on the Implementation of the Individuals with Disabilities Education Act (IDEA)* (U.S. Department of Education, 2002), available at: http://www2.ed.gov/about/reports/annual/osep/2002/index.html

---

SLD qualification has fallen from 50% to 39.2% while RTI and MTSS have gone up

The percentage of special education students qualified using SLD used to be about 50% of all students in special education. The usage of SLD peaked between 2000 and 2004, and has consistently been dropping since 2004. As of last available OSEP data (as this was written), Specific Learning Disability went from being 50% of all special education student to 39.2%. At the same time the usage of RTI and MTSS has increased. Is there anyone who believes that this is a coincidence? If we agree that this is not a coincidence, it is evidence that our belief systems were impacting our decisions, and still are, given that 39.2% is a very large number. We didn't just say let's put the kids into special education to get them some extra help, we said that the students had disabilities.

80% of referrals are about reading

We know that roughly 80% of students in special education have reading as a service, in many cases the primary service. We know that Dr. Carnine's meta-analysis

All Rights reserved by Steve Gill and Ushani Nanayakkara

of RTI/MTSS work shows that 70%-90% of the students we would like qualify for special education in the 2nd or 3rd grade are not in need of qualification after they receive appropriate interventions. We know from the work of Dr. Torgesen and the research on Lindamood Bell work, as high as 80% of the students with reading disabilities can be brought to grade level with short term intense intervention. We know that in many, possibly most cases, special education services within any given district encumbers upon general education funding (special education does not get enough money to pay its own bills).

So, what if a large number of students could be brought to grade level with the appropriate early interventions or short term intense interventions? We would not only save money, we would also have students finding more success. We mentioned earlier that the three top performing elementary schools in Kent have very low rates of special education qualification (and, these are not high SES schools). Also, a school district south of Kent was just recognized as having the fastest achievement gap closure in the state (they are also one of the only school districts using RTI as a districtwide method of special education qualification in Washington). These things cannot all be happening by chance!!!

The following information is taken from a presentation that Dr. Joseph Torgesen provided called "A Scientific Success Story: Specific Reading Disabilities or Developmental Dyslexia" at the Florida Council for Exceptional Children, October, 2006.

Dr. Torgesen reported on an intensive intervention provided for 60 students who had severe reading disabilities. The children were between 8 and 10 years of age. They had been receiving special education services for an average of 16 months. They were considered the worst readers and were on average at least 1.5 S.D. below grade level. They had standard scores of 69 for Word Attack, 69 for Word Identification and had Verbal IQs of 93 (average for each of these). These students were randomly assigned to two different groups and explicitly taught phonics skills. Both groups of students received 67.5 hours of one-to-one instruction, 2 hours per day for 8 weeks. The students were followed for two years after the intervention was completed.

All Rights reserved by Steve Gill and Ushani Nanayakkara

The results of the work are the following. The students not only gained skills that placed them in the average range, they actually continued to increase their reading skills after the intervention, scoring higher on standardized testing 2 years after the post intervention testing than at the post intervention testing. This means that they didn't just make initial gains, they didn't just maintain those gains, they improved relative to their peers over time.

Dr. Torgesen then asked the question, "How do we make this kind of instruction available to every child who needs it?" Imagine the positive impact on our children, both short-term and long-term, if we achieved this! Imagine the positive impacts on our classrooms if we achieved this!

9. Impact of Race on Qualification Rates

Does anyone still believe that people from different races have different rates of disabilities? When Steve was working on the over identification of Black/African American students as students with intellectual disabilities, he was told the following more than once: "Everyone knows that Black/African American students have lower average IQs, which means there will be more with IQs below 70, and that is why we have more qualified for Intellectual Disabilities." This is no joke, people really said that and believed that. Sadly, this type of thinking was exacerbated due to a book called The Bell Curve. This book supported ideas like this, and sadly encouraged people who wanted to believe things like this. Again, belief systems and acculturation have an impact on the way in which we see the world. For people who believe things like this (most of these people are good and caring people, just in need of some new knowledge), it is much easier to believe that their tests are an accurate representation if the results are poor. They are less likely to question their results and look for a different explanation/cause.

The quotes noted above show extreme disproportionality in our qualification rates of our Black/African American students. We say that we believe that the rate of disabilities do not differ by race, yet our qualification rates vary to the extreme for certain groups in certain categories. This is evidence that we need to examine our beliefs systems and acculturation. This is a complex topic, yet sincere and open conversations and reflection are needed to find our way to better results.

On a related note: Is race even a valid construct? This is a topic for many to discuss, but not a topic for this book. The term race is being used in this book for two reasons. First, it is used in all districts, all states, and at the national level for separating the students into groups. Second, we* use this construct to separate the students into groups. There is disproportionality across some groups and not others and the patterns of disproportionality are consistent. This is the problem. Yet this construct helps you know where to focus your efforts, once you know your numbers.

*We in this case is not the authors, but the school systems across the country.

One more related note is the discussion of cultural competency versus cultural responsiveness. As noted earlier, Steve usually uses Latino and Black. Someone asked Steve why he was doing this, questioning his cultural competence. Because of that Steve has added a discussion to all of his 1-day trainings. In education, there has been a great effort to make people culturally competent, which is something Steve and others question. The concept of cultural competence is based on a belief that we can look at someone and tell by their appearance what culture they identify with and then apply our knowledge of that culture. Steve uses Latino, given that his Spanish teacher uses the term Latino. However, he has talked to many people who could be Latina, Hispanic, Cubano, Peruana, Chicano, ... about this very topic. Roughly 40% of the people Steve talked to identified as Hispanic and 40% Latino, with 20% not identifying as either, but instead as Cubano, Peruana, Chicano, ... Also, Steve uses Black instead of African American, because two of his sons identify as Black, and not African American. Steve knows this because he asked them, independently, and they explained why they identify as Black and not African American. Steve also asked a co-worker the same question, and she identified as African American and explained why.

The point of this discussion is that we cannot know the cultural identity of someone by simply looking at them. Furthermore, even if we could, there are at least 400+ cultures within our schools (we have over 400 languages in our schools and that translates into well over 400 cultures), and we could not possibly know specific details about every one of these groups (even if we could identify people by their appearance). Instead, we need to be culturally responsive. We need to be careful in watching the people we work with. We need to watch their body language, have the courage to tell people that we need their help in understanding their culture, and have the courage to tell people that we might make mistakes and that we want them to educate us.

The following quote from the Center for Public Education is included to provide further evidence on this topic.

"The disparities between whites and some minorities in special education appear mostly in the categories with the most subjective eligibility criteria, such as "mild mental retardation" or "specific learning disabilities." Many believe the disproportionate representation is due to misconceptions about race and culture, and that black and Hispanic children are more likely to be misidentified as disabled (*Education Week* 2004, National Research Council 2002).

For instance, Matthew Ladner and Christopher Hammons argue that race plays an enormously important role in how students are identified as disabled (Ladner and Hammons, 2001). In a study in the book *Rethinking Special Education for a New Century,* they found that in districts with a predominantly black faculty, there was a reduction in minority student enrollment in special education services by three to four times. "Race," they concluded, "impacts special education rates far more than any other variable."

This examination of special education was prepared for the Center for Public Education by Ulrich Boser, October 15, 2009, available at:

http://www.centerforpubliceducation.org/Main-Menu/Evaluating-performance/Special-education-At-a-glance/Special-education-A-better-perspective-full-report.html

Did this chapter on Belief Systems and Acculturation change the way you look at this chart?

A snapshot of one district's data.... Percentage ELL qualified for special education by building

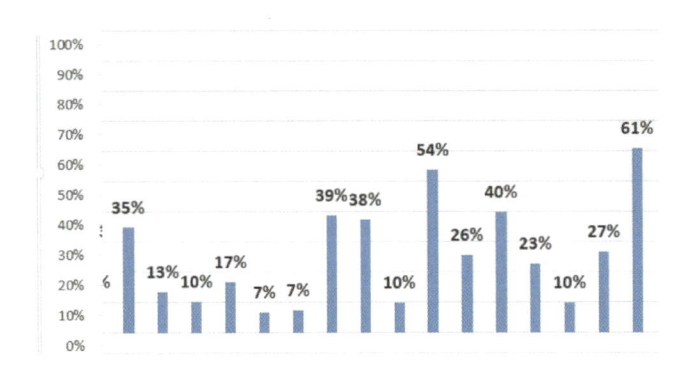

[Bar chart showing percentages by building: 35%, 13%, 10%, 17%, 7%, 7%, 39%, 38%, 10%, 54%, 26%, 40%, 23%, 10%, 27%, 61%]

ALL RIGHTS RESERVED BY STEVE GILL

Do you now see that it is likely that the results are based upon inappropriate qualifications? Can you see yourself as part of the solution?

"Takeaways"

1) We See What we are Acculturated to See: Real world examples of acculturation creating a lens. **We each need to examine the impact of our acculturation on our belief systems, on our practices, on our results.**

2) Steve's Personal Educator Journey: Real world example of developing over time, gaining new knowledge, changing practices. **Self-examination can be painful, but we need to figure out what we don't know, combine that with our acculturation, and remain lifelong learners, painful as it will be at times.**

All Rights reserved by Steve Gill and Ushani Nanayakkara

3) Steve Hirsh's and Walter Gilliam's Research: Research that shows the impact of our biases. **We all have biases, we need to examine how they are impacting our work, our results.**

4) Monolingual Nation: Real world examples that help us see what could be unrealistic expectations and/or a lack of reasonable expectations. **We expect our students, at times, to achieve very difficult tasks. Can we prove that we are creating structures that lead to good results for the vast majority of our students??? A student is not necessarily disabled if they are struggling in a system in which 20% or more of the students are struggling!!!**

5) Literacy and Intelligence: Knowledge to help us see things differently. **We need to have knowledge to determine how things are related, correlated. Without this, we can make judgments that have no validity.**

6) Poverty: Research that show our results, and indicates biases. **This is more evidence that our biases, beliefs, acculturation impact our results. The more we know about where our problems are, the better we can focus on fixing our problems.**

7) Qualification vs Disability: Research that shows our results do not follow logical patterns, nor our "spoken" beliefs. **We need to examine our results and the results in our district, in order to understand where to begin our introspection, and where and how to change our practices.**

8) Reading and Referrals: Research that indicates our system, results and beliefs have significant flaws. **There are methods out there that lead to different results. This shows us that many of the students we believe have disabilities are just not getting their needs met. What are we going to do?**

9) Race vs Disability: Research that shows our results, again, do not follow logical patterns, nor our "spoken" beliefs. **Again, our results do not match what we say that we believe. We need to examine our acculturation, belief systems and practices to achieve better results. No shame, no blame.**

Closing Thoughts On Belief Systems

During the editing of this book, the question was asked, "How do you change what people believe?" As educators, we are caring individuals. The problems, or poor results, within disproportionality are not occurring due to individuals purposefully doing harmful things to children. As educators see the impact of their actions or inactions in this area they will be highly motivated to change the results. Working on belief systems and acculturation, although painful at times, will be something that they do. Knowing that belief systems are a combination of acculturation and knowledge, educators will look for the knowledge they need (some of which can be found in Steve's and Ushani's books) and other information contained in the books of many individuals we refer to within our books. Then, you can use the processes within Steve's and Ushani's books to change practices, which lead to changes in results.

John Hattie is possibly the leading expert in the world on what is and is not effective within educational strategies (Hattie's books, like <u>Visible Learning</u>, are powerful and useful books to own). An effect size of .4 is basically what is expected, the .9 is a very large effect size, and the 1.57 and 1.62 are extremely large effect sizes. The following are some examples are found within his books or through Google searches:

.19 for Co/Team Teaching

.47 for Small Group Learning

.53 for Scaffolding

.90 for Teacher Credibility

1.57 for Collective Teacher Belief

1.62 for Teacher Expectations of Student Performance

It is easy to see from this that beliefs have extremely powerful effects on our results. Also, having the knowledge, like that provided by Hattie, can sure save a lot of time, time that could be wasted on practices that are proven to have low impact on student learning.

Anthony Muhammad, author of several books, wrote the following in his book *Overcoming the Achievement Gap Trap*, "We cannot solve the problem until we look at it differently (page 61)" and "We cannot pursue equality when our value systems favor one group over another, especially when we lack the courage to even discuss the problem objectively (page 75)."

The work by Carol Dweck and her book on growth mindset versus fixed mindset is fantastic information for anyone in the process of evaluating and working on their own beliefs. It is also a great book for book study groups and the valuable discussions that can occur during book studies.

You have seen the problems, the issues about acculturation and belief systems, their impact on practice and results. It will take courage and knowledge to move forward. The good news is that better results lead to higher levels of satisfaction, so it will be worth it.

Chapter 7: Examples for Special Education Evaluation Reports

The following paragraphs provide language you may use in writing content for intervention plans, referral documents and/or special education evaluation reports.

Each of these examples covers just one possible piece of data that could be collected related to the item number and are meant to encourage thinking on the topic. These are clearly not all inclusive.

For a few items we included ELL student specific examples to provoke thinking and provide examples of wording. **Those are in green.** If the team is trying to better understand the needs of an ELL student, the ELL Critical Data Process is needed in place of this process.

Important notes are in red.

Item # 1 Examples (Exposure)

The student is struggling with appropriate behavior in kindergarten, and it is September.

Example that supports intervention:

Johnny wanders around the classroom when the other students are lined up and ready to leave the classroom (e.g., to go to the music class). Johnny did not attend a preschool setting and is a first born child. Johnny was well socialized by his parents, with neighborhood children and relatives. However, Johnny has not had exposure to situations in which the expectation would have been to line up with other children in order to transition to a new activity.

Example that could support a referral:

Johnny wanders around the classroom when the other students are lined up and ready to leave the classroom (e.g., to go to the music class). Johnny attended preschool for two years prior to entering kindergarten. Johnny's preschool teachers reported that Johnny was exposed to children following the routine of lining up for transitions, but he usually needed one-to-one support to get to the line, to know where to stand, and to stay in line.

Item # 2 Examples (Experience)

Example that supports intervention:

Henry is a student with autism who demonstrates strong academic skills (on standardized tests). His teachers and family are concerned that, although the academic skills are clearly present, he does not produce at standard within the classroom setting. Henry's experience has been that he was given passing grades each year due to the knowledge that he does understand the work, and just is not producing. Henry prefers to play with the toys on his desk, but when working with the teacher he demonstrates that he fully understands the assignments. Staff are working with the family to create a reward system at school that will include rewards at home, and the system will focus on completing work to a standard that demonstrates the core skills (noting that at this time Henry is unlikely to go above this standard, even with rewards).

Example that could support a referral:

Henry is a student with autism who demonstrates strong academic skills (on standardized tests). His teachers and family are concerned that, although the academic skills are clearly present, he does not produce at standard within the classroom setting. Henry has been on multiple plans to improve his production and multiple accommodations have been provided. Henry's disability is now appearing to adversely impact his access to his education. That is, even though he has many academic skills, he is not demonstrating the ability to apply those skills and testing is indicating the he is losing ground to his peers academically.

Item # 3 Examples (Expectations)

Example that supports intervention:

Suzy is a three-and-a-half-year-old girl whose speech is virtually unintelligible. Within the home setting, Suzy's parents and older siblings virtually always attempt to guess what she wants and allow her to "grunt" to confirm what it is that she wants and does not want. There is not an expectation placed on Suzy to approximate the correct words, and therefore she does not practice the correct words. The SLP will work with the family to create a home plan that will create the expectation that Suzy attempt to copy the correct words and that she is reinforced for closer and closer approximations.

Example that could support a referral:

Suzy is a three and a half- year-old girl whose speech is virtually unintelligible. Within the home setting, Suzy's parents and older siblings provide Suzy modelling for the words she is attempting to say, Suzy always attempts these words, yet nobody outside the immediate family can understand what Suzy is attempting to say. After interviewing the family and listening to Suzy, the SLP recommends a referral as the next step.

Item # 4 Examples (Practice)

Example that supports intervention:

Andre is a student of Northern European heritage who is struggling greatly in school. All of the data collected supports a referral for Andre, and the school psychologist learns that the parents place a great deal of pressure on the children to learn their native language, expect the girls to do well in school, yet are not concerned about their boys learning or performing in English. Andre's current teacher and previous teacher state that he does not complete much of the school work. Therefore, Andre has been exposed to English for 6 years, has experienced direct instruction in English, but his parents have no concerns nor expectations regarding his performance or learning in English. Andre therefore

All Rights reserved by Steve Gill and Ushani Nanayakkara

completes as little work (practice) as possible within the school. The school staff meets with the family to discuss the impact this is having on Andre and the possible future impact.

Example that could support a referral:

Andrea (Andre's sister) is a student of Northern European heritage who is struggling greatly in school. The school psychologist interviews the family and learns that the family puts a great deal of pressure on the children to learn the family's native language and expects the girls to also do well in their English learning. Andrea has a long history of completing all classroom work (practice), yet continues to do poorly in school. Andrea has been exposed to learning in English for 6 years, she has experienced the same opportunities as her older sister (who is doing well in school), and her parents expect and support her learning in English. The team, using this data and data from the ELL Critical Data Process, determine that a special education referral is an appropriate action at this time.

Item # 5 Examples (Attendance History)

Important Note: The definition of what is poor attendance or attendance that is truly at risk attendance may already be defined within your school district. Also, there is a large body of work on early warning systems for failure or dropout risk. Chicago Public Schools was an early leader in this area. We (the authors) are using 3 days of unexcused absences per year and/or 15 days of combined absences.

Example that supports intervention:

Layla has 2 unexcused absences and 12 total absences as of March 15th of the current school year. Layla has a long history of absences per school year. Layla's mother leaves for work very early and Layla is expected to get up and go to school by herself. If Layla sleeps-in in the morning she tends to stay at home. Also, Layla struggles in preparing breakfast for herself. The school has purchased an alarm clock for Layla and is working with Layla and her mother regarding easy to make breakfast ideas.

Example that could support a referral:

Layla only has one absence this school year as of April 15th. Layla has a long history of strong attendance, yet she has always struggled in school. The combination of strong attendance and poor academic success is one piece of data that supports a potential special education referral.

ELL specific discussion:

Example that supports intervention:

May has missed a great deal of school this year.* Our school has a 98% attendance rate and only 0.5% of the students have either 3 unexcused absences or more than 9 total absences. When May was interviewed, it was clear that she was missing school due to a lack of understanding that attendance is required. May and the principal discussed this at length, and May was unaware of this as an expectation.

* Give the actual number of days when you write it.

Example that could support a referral:

Lin has missed a great deal of school this year. * Our school has a 98% attendance rate and only 0.5% of the students have either 3 unexcused absences or more than 9 total absences. When Lin was interviewed, it was made clear that the high absenteeism is due to not believing that school is a place where success can be found. Lin's parents noted that Lin has struggled far more in school than their other children, and that absenteeism has always been a problem.

* Give the actual number of days when you write it.

Focus on whether or not the absenteeism is related to school being hard for the student in general (historically), as opposed to learning English and performing in

All Rights reserved by Steve Gill and Ushani Nanayakkara

English being hard for the student. This is where parent and student interviews, with a strong emphasis on historical performance and sibling comparisons, is very important.

Item # 6 Examples (Intervention Description)

Example that supports intervention:

Jeff, a second grade student, has received an intervention for phoneme awareness with a group of 4 other students who have also demonstrated a need for an intervention in this area. All of the students received pre-tests, post-tests and ongoing progress monitoring during the intervention. The growth curves for each of the students was graphed, and Jeff's growth curve was the second strongest of the five students during this intervention. Therefore, the team will continue general education reading interventions with Jeff at this time.

Example that could support a referral:

Jeff, a second grade student, has received an intervention for phoneme awareness with a group of 4 other students who have also demonstrated a need for an intervention in this area. All of the students received pre-tests, post-tests and ongoing progress monitoring during the intervention. The growth curves for each of the students was graphed, and Jeff's growth curve was the lowest of the five students. Not only that, the other students' growth curves were similar and Jeff's growth curve represented far less progress than the other students. Therefore, the team agreed that this data is supportive of a special education referral.

ELL Specific Discussion:

This is a critical item, especially when the student does not reach the 5-7 year threshold (Jim Cummins, a leader in this field of work, states that his evidence indicates it takes an English Language Learner 5-7 years to become competitive). The team needs to examine how the student of concern responded to an intervention that was targeted to the specific need, and was provided for a minimum of 10 weeks with intensity and fidelity. It is important to be able to document how the team knows for sure that the intervention actually targeted the specific need of the student of concern (no guessing, actual facts). Then, look at the growth curves. A growth curve similar to that of the other students with similar needs (and similar language learning backgrounds) indicates that seeking qualification under the category of Specific Learning Disability is likely not the appropriate decision. A growth curve significantly below that of other students with similar needs and language backgrounds is indicative of a need to make a special education referral.

Student whose data is not supportive of a referral:

Alexandria was provided a targeted intervention in the area of reading, more specifically phonemic awareness skills. This area was chosen based upon the universal screening completed by the school. Alexandria demonstrated the lowest skills in this area for a second grade student. Alexandria was grouped with three other students who demonstrated the same concern and who are all language learners. Two of these students speak the same native language as Alexandria: one has been learning English slightly longer and one has been learning English for a slightly shorter period of time. Alexandria's skills in this area were measured before the intervention, 4 times during the intervention, and 3 days after the intervention was completed. Alexandria's rate of growth on this intervention was similar to that of the other 3 students. In fact, she had the strongest growth curve of the four students.

Student whose data is supportive of a special education referral:

Alexio was provided a targeted intervention in the area of reading, more specifically phonemic awareness skills. This area was chosen based upon the universal screening completed by the school, where Alexio demonstrated the lowest skills in this area for a second grade student. Alexio was grouped with three other students who demonstrated the same concern and who are all language learners. Two of these students speak the same native language as Alexio: one has been learning English slightly longer and one has been learning English for a slightly shorter period of time. One student does not speak the same language as Alexio, but speaks a language that has roughly the same

All Rights reserved by Steve Gill and Ushani Nanayakkara

number of native speakers in the district and he has been learning English for the same length of time as Alexio. Alexio's skills in this area were measured before the intervention, as well as 4 times during the intervention, and 3 days after the intervention was completed. Alexio's rate of growth on this intervention was the slowest rate of growth of the 4 students and was significantly below the rate of growth of the other three students (who all demonstrated similar rates of growth).

Item # 7 Examples (Expectations in general education classroom)

Example that supports intervention:

Lisa has been at Alpha Elementary for three years and is currently in the fourth grade. Lisa is a quiet and compliant little girl who is very well liked by her teachers. Lisa's teachers have consistently been concerned with regards to her skills, and due to this they have placed very low expectations on Lisa's performance and work completion. Therefore, the team is going to plan for higher level expectations for Lisa and design a support system both within the school and at home for Lisa to complete more classroom work with higher expectations and support. The team will monitor this to measure Lisa's growth as this occurs and increase the expectations as Lisa's skills grow.

Example that could support a referral:

Lisa has been at Alpha Elementary for three years and is currently in the fourth grade. Lisa is a quiet and compliant little girl who is very well liked by her teachers. Lisa's teachers have consistently been concerned with regards to her skills. They have consistently placed high expectations on Lisa's academic performance and they supported her in her attempts to complete the work at the level of their expectations. Even with this level of expectation and support, and even with Lisa attempting to complete the work to the best of her ability, she is not demonstrating growth at expected levels, when compared to peers.

All Rights reserved by Steve Gill and Ushani Nanayakkara

Important note: with a student who is struggling, high expectations might still mean modifying (lowering) the criteria. For example, for a student who has missed learning time (e.g. too many moves), the expectations may be high and may still not be grade level expectations. The goal is to have the student working hard, with support, at a level that can either demonstrate reasonable growth (all things considered) or that demonstrates a student not making expected levels of growth (all things considered).

ELL specific discussion:

If the student has not been required to turn in homework at all times in which other students have had the requirement, then the team should lean toward more interventions. If the student has had the requirement and made an effort at all times, yet there has been little progress or growth, then the team should lean toward a special education referral.

Student whose data is not supportive of a referral:

Cindy is a student in Mr. Jones' classroom. During observation, the students in Mr. Jones' classroom are on-task approximately 65% of the time. Also, the observer who did not know Cindy, was unable to pick Cindy out from the other students when completing a "blind" observation. Upon completing a second observation, and knowing who Cindy was from the beginning of the observation, the data indicated that Cindy is on-task the same percentage of time as other students in the classroom. When Mr. Jones was interviewed, he stated that Cindy does not turn in many of her assignments, and he guessed that she turned in approximately 50% of her work. Mr. Jones was unsure; given that he sometimes gives Cindy a passing grade on an assignment when she participates in the classroom without disrupting. This indicates that the integrity of the grades limits the ability to use the grades as evidence.

Most of our examples are about what is supportive of a referral or supportive of more interventions. This example; however, is about a situation in which the teacher has, through their actions, made it impossible for the team to determine the meaning of the data for classroom expectations. The teacher has been inconsistent and has graded work in a manner that does not measure work quality. An environment with appropriate expectations allows the team to evaluate the skills development of the student to understand how the student learns. The environment created by this teacher did not allow the team to use skills development or a lack of skills development (meaning no measurable improvement of skills by the student) to understand how the student learns.

Student whose data is supportive of a referral:

Jimmy is a student in Mrs. Johnson's classroom. Mrs. Johnson's classroom is a well-run classroom. Her students are on task, as measured during observations, 94% of the time. Also, the state test scores for Mrs. Johnson's students are consistently above those of 3rd grade students across the school district. In Mrs. Johnson's classroom, Jimmy is expected to complete assignments when other students are expected to complete assignments. Mrs. Johnson, knowing Jimmy struggles in school, began the school year allowing Jimmy to complete the assignments at a lower level than other students, while supporting Jimmy and raising the expectations consistently. Jimmy has made some growth over time with respect to completing assignments that are closer to the rubrics Mrs. Johnson has for her students. However, Jimmy's work is still at the lowest level of the students in Mrs. Johnson's classroom.

Item # 8 Examples (Classroom Observation)

Important Note: The classroom observations should be marked, within the matrix, from neutral to referral. If a student has a lack of positive response to intervention, that will be addressed within the matrix in areas other than the classroom observation. Therefore, this item is going to either reflect a student who is not performing during the observation (meaning a mark of neutral, given there is no way to know if a lack of interaction is due to a lack of desire, confusion about what the assignment is, or confusion regarding how to complete

the assignment). A student who is actively trying to do what is expected but having no success should receive a mark toward referral in the matrix.

Example that could support a referral:

Louis, when observed in Mrs. Smith's classroom, was carefully observing what other students were doing and attempting to complete the task, yet he was having no success. Mrs. Smith reported, as did Louis's previous teacher, that Louis consistently attempts all work in the classroom and rarely completes any of the classroom work to the grade level standards.

Item # 9 Examples (Comparison Student Data)

Example that supports more intervention:

Johnny was compared to 4 of his classmates in his PE class regarding how quickly he learns new games/sports, both the rules and the skills. Johnny is considered an average athlete by both his PE teacher and his parents, and this comparison was not about physical ability, but learning the rules and learning the parts of the skills. Johnny's PE teacher rated Johnny in comparison to the other 4 students twice per week for a total of 8 weeks, and she did not know which one of the students was the student of concern. She rated each of the students on a 1 to 5 scale (one meaning struggles to learn the rules and skills to 5 learning the rules and skills quickly). At the end of the 8 weeks, Johnny's average was the second highest average of the group of students.

Example that supports a referral:

Johnny was compared to 4 of his classmates in his PE class regarding how quickly he learns new games/sports, both the rules and the skills. Johnny is considered an average athlete by both his PE teacher and by his parents, and this comparison was not about physical ability, but learning the rules and learning the parts of the skills. Johnny's PE teacher rated Johnny in comparison to the other 4 students twice per week for a total of 8 weeks, and she did not know which one of the students was the student of concern. She rated each of the students on a 1 to 5 scale (one meaning struggles to learn the rules and skills to 5 learning the rules and skills quickly). At the end of the 8 weeks, Johnny's average was the lowest average of the group of students. The school psychologist interviewed the PE teacher regarding Johnny's performance in her classroom, and she stated that he works hard, carefully watches the other students to mimic their actions, but still struggles greatly to understand what is expected of him.

Item # 10 Examples (Poverty)

Important Note: There is not a specific school based intervention that is related to poverty and skills development in relationship to this matrix based process. Instead, the staff completing this need to examine the potential impacts of the poverty and design interventions if there is a noted likely impact of the poverty. That is, poverty in and of itself does not have a meaningful relationship to disability. However, poverty could have an impact on exposure to activities and/or experiences that help to prepare students for school. If there is evidence of a lack of exposure and/or experience related to poverty the mark goes toward intervention and if there is no evidence of this the mark should be placed as neutral. The intervention should focus on activities related to filling noted gaps in exposure and/or experience.

Item # 11 Examples (Behavior)

Example that supports intervention:

Stephanie is a student whose parents are currently in the process of getting a divorce. The parents have confirmed that the process has been very difficult on the children and the children have heard things that the parents wish the children had not heard. In addition, Stephanie's little brother is in the process of receiving treatment for cancer. Stephanie's behavior within the school setting is very problematic, and the school and the family see a clear relationship between the events in her life and her behavior. The parents are arranging outside counseling for Stephanie. Within the school setting, the school is arranging plans to help Stephanie when she is not demonstrating the ability to manage her behaviors. For example, if the behaviors are relatively minor in nature, Stephanie can use the quiet area within the classroom setting and return to class activities when she is ready. For more significant behaviors, Stephanie will be instructed to go to the school counselor's office. Stephanie will be given time to do activities that have been shown to calm her. Then, Stephanie will complete an activity with the counselor that allows her to process what occurred and what she could have done in the classroom that would have been more appropriate.

Example that could support a referral:

Stephen is demonstrating behaviors within the classroom that are adversely impacting his ability to access his education. That is, Stephen is either not engaged in the learning activity or has been removed from the classroom due to his behavior. The interviews with the family indicate that there are struggles within the home setting, but that these struggles are due to mental health issues of the parents. The psychologist working with the family has diagnosed Stephen with Bipolar Disorder. The team is concerned that Stephen's behavior is due to this medical condition and that his behavior is adversely impacting his access to his education.

Item # 12 Examples (Trauma)

Important Note: It is rare that trauma is something that can be treated within the school setting. This is changing in some areas, though. However, if there is a student with a clear history of trauma, the school can help the parents follow through on seeking trauma treatment for the student. Therefore, for this item, the team will mark neutral if there is no evidence of trauma. If there is evidence of trauma, the team will place the mark toward more intervention and hopefully be able to help the family find potential resources.

Item # 13 Examples (Parent Interview)

Important Note: This item is scored by the team based upon the totality of data during the parent interview when looking at things like: student learning history, parental learning history and sibling learning history.

Example that supports intervention:

Joseph has demonstrated the ability to learn new material, his parents have reported that there are no adult family members with a history of learning difficulties, and Joseph's two older siblings have done well in school. The current struggles that Joseph is having in school are new struggles. The team is unsure at this time why Joseph is struggling during the current school year, and the team has decided to provide Joseph academic interventions in math (the area of concern) while trying to better understand the root cause of the current struggles.

Example that could support a referral:

Joselyn has demonstrated a history of core academic deficits. Her parents have reported that school was difficult for them, and her mother reported that she received special education services when she was in school. Joselyn's older brother has a learning disability and is receiving special education services. This information is seen by the team as data that supports a potential special education referral.

ELL Specific Content:

The goal for the interviews is to learn whether or not something critical has not otherwise been considered. Is there a medical condition that was not noted that needs to be considered? Is there a family history of learning difficulties?

Student whose data is supportive of intervention:

Stephanie's parents reported that she met developmental milestones at the same rate as her siblings and cousins. They noted that there is no history of learning problems within any of the family members and that Stephanie has had no injuries or illness of any significance.

All Rights reserved by Steve Gill and Ushani Nanayakkara

Examples of students whose data is supportive of a referral:

1. Xavier's parents stated during the parent interview that many of the family members have found school to be very difficult. They noted that although their friends were learning to read well in school, they had had many difficulties learning to read. Also, Xavier demonstrated more difficult time learning his age appropriate self-help skills as compared to his cousins.

2. David's parents stated that they had had many doctors' appointments in their home country when David was a child. They stated that the doctors had told them that David would have a more difficult time learning and that school would be difficult for him, due to the medical problems. The family was unsure of the diagnosis, but stated they had paperwork in their native language that might have the information. The school psychologist made a copy of the paperwork, and worked with a trained interpreter/translator to both talk with the family and translate the documents. The translator was asked to look for any medical diagnoses and any statements regarding the possible impacts of the medical conditions. The translator provided the school psychologist with a list of medical diagnoses documented in the paperwork and the statements by the doctors regarding the possible impact on learning.

Item # 14 Examples (Developmental History)

Example that supports intervention:

Lisa's parents have reported that she met all of her developmental milestones and was talking at an early age. Lisa's parents report that she did not have any significant illnesses, injuries, or fevers as a child. This information is seen by the team as supporting the need to provide Lisa further interventions in the areas of concern.

Example that could support a referral:

Robert's parents have reported that he walked and talked at a much later age than his brothers and sisters. Robert's parents have reported that he had many illnesses as a child, and they have documents at home that explain the illnesses. The parents are going to bring the documents to the school, and the school will make copies of these documents for the family. The team has determined that this information is supportive of a special education referral.

Important Note: This is a good place to remind you that each item is one factor within the series of factors inside the matrix. Sometimes people get stressed over taking information, like above, and saying it is supportive of a referral. Remember, a referral will not lead to an evaluation unless there is an abundance of data indicating that a special education evaluation is the appropriate action.

Chapter 8: Special Education Categories: Problem areas

The reality is that most referrals lead to evaluations and most evaluations lead to qualification. This can be a good thing or this can be a bad thing. If your team has done a great job of evaluating your data, and the data shows proportional qualification and strong intervention systems (i.e., low % qualified for special education services and high test scores), then referrals leading to evaluations and to qualification (in most cases) means that your team is doing a great job in referring, testing, and qualifying the students who truly have disabilities that are adversely impacting their education and need something "special." Without that strong intervention and pre-referral process, your team is just going be guessing once it is time to make the decision regarding whether or not to qualify the student for special education services. Guessing might be strong language, but at the minimum the confidence of your team in its decisions will vary greatly.

The purpose of this chapter is to help you understand that the majority of disproportionality occurs within certain disability categories and the disproportionality tends to also be specific to race or linguistic group.

The Language Learner examples are included in order to provide the reader additional examples of ways in which to look at and examine evaluations. If the student is a language learner, the ELL Critical Data Process should be used to determine whether more interventions or a referral is the appropriate action to take.

"Hard" Categories: First Group of Eligibility Categories in Which There is Little or No Disproportionality

By any chance, are we evaluating a student who happens to possibly be eligible in one of the "hard" categories? The "hard" categories are the more concrete in nature categories and it is likely that neither language acquisition nor race nor poverty are a defining characteristic. For example, children with blindness or deafness are highly likely to need special education services, and their race and/or linguistic history are unlikely to be major factors in qualification or not.

Therefore, we are not including any extra discussion regarding these categories:

- Hearing Impairment or Deafness
- Visual Impairment (including Blindness)
- Orthopedic Impairment
- Traumatic Brain Injury
- Deaf-Blind
- Multiple Disabilities
- Autism

Good news: the above categories represent at least 50% of the categories.

Second Group: Problems Exist and Vary by Race or Linguistic History

The eligibility categories in this group are more difficult to analyze, yet are not as extreme as the final two groups. They are more difficult in this context due to the impacts of language learning, acculturation issues, poverty issues, and more. Additionally, historical issues of over-qualification of language learners and certain racial groups within intellectual disability might have impacted the way in which educators think about this category (i.e., some people might believe that certain groups have higher rates of intellectual disabilities).

Each of these disability categories has its own unique issues and problems, with the first disability category often having historical under qualification for language learners and the second and third disability categories having historical over qualification for certain racial groups.

- Other Health Impairment

- Intellectual Disability
- Emotional/Behavioral Disability

Other Health Impairment

The issue here tends to be under qualification for language learners. In many cases, this appears to be caused by the difficulties the families face in navigating our medical system whereas our families in poverty could be struggling with medical coverage issues. These struggles often lead to under identification in this category. And, from what Steve has seen from many districts, the students who are struggling are then placed into the Specific Learning Disability category.

This category tends to be easier in the terms of qualification, if one can get the needed documentation. It is important to note that the laws place the responsibility on the district to obtain any information that it believes necessary to appropriately qualify a student. That is a very tricky responsibility to navigate and staff really need to work with their administrative teams to travel that road.

If you have the needed documentation, the process is reasonably simple. In any of these cases, the team needs to determine the relationship between the noted condition, the adverse impact on the student to accessing their education (with and without language impact) and whether or not the student needs special education (specially designed instruction that is not dependent upon impacts of language acquisition) in order to access their education. If language learning was not an issue, would the medical condition by itself be creating this adverse impact? To the same extent?

Intellectual Disability for Language Learners

Sadly, when teams do not know what to do, they may default to pushing these hard to identify students into the Specific Learning Disability category through inappropriate application of the legal term "professional judgment." If your team is facing this tough decision, there are ways to look at the data and come to a better decision.

In addition, adaptive behavior scales are normed on what we believe is appropriate development in these areas (given the normative sample). In many cases you will get results that are either totally useless or of such questionable use that you cannot use them to determine if there are potential disability issues versus issues that are culturally based issues. Therefore, if you must use an adaptive behavior measure (and sometimes you are required to based upon the laws), you really need to get to know more about the exposure, experiences, expectations and practice history of the student.

For example, for a student who is unable to (or just does not) feed themselves (according to the rating scale), have they ever been asked/required to do so? Or, for a student who cannot put on a jacket by themselves, did they live in an area in which the weather didn't require the use of jackets? Or, for a student who cannot tie their own shoes, do they have shoes without laces? Keep going with this line of logic for any question in which a student is not demonstrating a skill, just in case they had limited exposure/experience/expectations/practice.

Then, start asking about the daily life of the student in their previous environment. It is possible you are going to find out that they can do something rather difficult that many people "here" could not do (e.g., start a fire without matches, hunt/fish with limited resources, etcetera). In the end, you must take into account the relationship of exposure/experience/expectation/practice to actual performance. It is unfair to consider a student impaired for something they have never had exposure/experience/expectation/practice with, or that it was very limited. For example, considering a student to have fine motor issue with a pencil when they only just started to use one would be inappropriate. Also, it would be unfair to neglect the skills a student has that are not measured on our rating skills. In the end, though, the team will need to make a determination based on exposure/experience/expectations/practice: does this student actually have an impairment or not?

Emotional Behavioral Disability for Language Learners

In order to make this decision, you need to be able to rule-out a lot of issues.

First, is the student's bad behavior (we would not be looking at this category if bad behavior was not present) actually the cause of the adverse impact on their access to their education? Or, is the lack of ability to communicate needs and wants creating bad behavior (due to frustration)? You are only going to be able to analyze this if you have the data very well documented for your school and district. In other words, how many of your ELL students are demonstrating problem behaviors and to what degree? What percentage of your ELL students are finding academic success? How does that rate compare to research on effective ELL programs (look into the work of Dr. Collier and Dr. Thomas, if you have not already done so).

Second, is the student a student who needs support for trauma? If there is a history of trauma, and it is untreated, you might provide support for the student that is of little or no value. No quantity of the wrong intervention leads to good results.

Third, what is the relationship of academic struggles to the noted behavior? That is, if a student is behaving poorly to hide academic struggles then the intervention needed is much different than if the bad behaviors are causing academic struggles.

Last, is there a cultural issue that is not being addressed? The majority of students qualified in this category are boys and some of our boys are coming from cultures that have a very different outlook in general and sometimes specifically in male/female power relationships. This is a difficult area to address, but we do not want to label a child as disabled due to struggles they are having with cultural differences.

Third Group: Disproportionality Can Increase for Language Learners and Children in Poverty

Many of the problems in these two categories are caused by good people just wanting to help and at some level ignoring the fact that the student is being labeled as having a disability. Many of the issues within these two categories are caused by staff members not knowing the history of the student or the characteristics of the language of the student well enough to understand the root problem. Knowing the data within your school and district is critical to knowing if you are facing a problem regarding belief systems in your district.

- Speech or Language Impairment
- Developmental Delay

Speech or Language Impairment

There are two main areas that create concerns: language (expressive and receptive) and articulation. Within the area of language, there are times in which grammar becomes an issue. This tends to ignore the information that exists on the development of language for a second or later language for the student. Even for students who are simultaneous bilinguals, usually one of the languages is not as strong as the other language and will continue to have some grammar issues, possibly throughout life. For students who are sequential bilinguals, mastering certain aspects of grammar may take a lifetime or just may not occur at all. For anyone who is learning Spanish, reaching a near 100% correct usage of "por" and "para" just may never occur. For someone coming from Spanish to English, mastering when to use "in" versus "on" can take a lifetime. I am using the English and Spanish examples given my experience with them, but also because 75% of our ELLs are Spanish to English learners (at last check this was 67% in Washington, and 85% in California).

When an SLP is considering a student for qualification in the category of Speech or Language Impairment, they need to have a strong knowledge of the student's language acquisition history and knowledge about that language within the community. In Steve's experience across many districts, a certain pattern occurs: not all of the languages are represented within the special education student group, and for some languages, students are only qualified in those "hard" categories. For example, the Kent School District normally has 130 to 140 languages spoken. However, we usually only have 40-45 of those languages represented within our special education student population. This is, in part, due to sample sizes (some of the languages only have 1-2 speakers and you should not expect to see a student within all of those groups).

However, that does not explain the size of the difference. Also, some languages are over-represented and the patterns of the over-representation are consistent. Spanish tends to be over represented for language (expressive and receptive) and some Asian languages are over represented for articulation. So, once a therapist knows this information, they can then talk to people about the usage of the language in the community (especially for the high incidence languages). The bottom line here is to determine whether or not the student in question for qualification in language actually needs English when they leave the school setting (or even needs it within the school setting). For example, can the student travel within the school or community and only use very little English? If this is the case, then the apparent needs/adverse impact of the student in English would need to be extreme to justify qualification, and, the student would need to demonstrate significant issues within their native language (according to multiple speakers of that language). Without this, we would be qualifying students simply because they do not practice something that really is not that important in their life: English. Additionally, their exposure might be limited within and outside the school.

What about articulation? The therapist really needs to know about the structure of the language, whether or not the sounds of English are present within the language of the student, and the developmental norms for that language. It is inappropriate to qualify a student for articulation issues when the sounds that are creating the problematic score do not exist in the primary language of the student or are not yet developmentally expected in the student's native language.

Confusion occurs with staff around the concept of "adverse impact" and the words adverse impact. The concept "adverse impact" is about how a disability creates an adverse impact on the child's ability to access their education and requires special education services; it is not just about the simple fact that the child is doing poorly in school. The confusion stems from staff thinking that adverse impact is synonymous with doing poorly in school. However, doing poorly in school could be related to the many other issues discussed in this book, and could have no relationship to a disability. If a child is not yet in school, adverse impact means a disability is the cause of a child's delayed development of developmentally appropriate daily living/activities skills (e.g., communication skills, motor skills, adaptive behavior skills).

The following charts are used by SLPs to help parents understand the developmental ages related to sounds/blends, the first chart is for English and the second for Spanish. Trying to find this same information for other languages becomes more difficult as the languages become less commonly used. And, we have over 400 languages spoken in our schools in the United States. It takes work to find out the developmentally appropriate ages and the differences in sounds across these 400+ languages, but that is needed to know whether or not your evaluation of the student has any validity or usefulness.

English

Developmental Articulation Norms –

AGES

4	5	7	7.5	8.5
m	k	v	r	z
h	d	-ing	l	th (the)
n	g		s	th (with)
w	f		ch	
b	y		sh	
p	t		j	
			/r/ blends	
			/s/ blends	
			/l/ blends	

Based on: Massachusetts Speech and Hearing Association Entrance and Exit Criteria Guidelines
90% mastery

All Rights reserved by Steve Gill and Ushani Nanayakkara

Spanish Developmental Articulation Norms -

AGES

3	4	5	6	7
m	k	d	x	rr
b	l	g	s	
p	w	ñ		
	f	r		
	y	ch		
	t			
	n			

Based on: Jimenez 1987, Acevedo 1993
90% mastery

Developmental Delay for Language Learners

The category Developmental Delay consists of five subcategories: Social or Emotional, Adaptive, Communication, Cognitive and Motor (Physical Development).

This category could be the category in which exposure/experience/expectations/practice are the most critical. You will be trying to determine whether or not a young child/student who is coming to you from poverty or with language differences, and probably cultural differences, has a disability that impacts their access to their general daily activities. The Preschool Version of the ELL Critical Data Process focuses on understanding these issues for preschool age language learners. In the end, your team will need to determine whether or not, regardless of the score, the student had a real opportunity to grow the skill in question like a student who was within the normative sample. Remember that the category Developmental Delay is a category of special education. Therefore, the team may indicate a belief that the student is likely to have a

All Rights reserved by Steve Gill and Ushani Nanayakkara

disability, which may be accurate, or that the delay may respond to intervention (meaning no disability). To know if your school and district is doing this well, you must know what percentage of these students is found no longer eligible for special education, what percentage continues to qualify for special education and your overall rate of special education qualification. Analyze your evaluations of your previously DD qualified students to see the results of those evaluations. What percentage are continued within special education? And, in what categories? The team needs to know the percentage of language learners who continue versus the percentage of non-language learners, to analyze their decision making and service delivery.

Developmental Delay for Non Language Learners

This tends to revolve around issues that are related to social-emotional, adaptive behavior and/or communication. More "extreme" issues like significant medical problems or significant cognitive issues should not be the issue when this category is the center of the discussion. This means, do not qualify students as developmentally delayed when you have evidence of a disability that is clearly lifelong in nature.

<u>Exposure, Experience, Expectations and Practice must be examined</u>.

Social/emotional issues: The team must integrate their information from before and during the referral process to their data obtained during the evaluation process if an evaluation is recommended and completed. Based on that information, can the team state that social-emotional issues exist to the extent that, after subtracting out issues with exposure/experience/ expectations/ and/or practice, there would still be a large enough problem/concern that qualification is the appropriate step?

Adaptive behavior: When the team is looking at adaptive behavior, they must go through a similar process, answering the same basic questions. Additionally, they must be able to come to the conclusion that, after subtracting out language and culture (if there are applicable issues), the student would still have significant impacts within adaptive behavior that are directly, or primarily related to delayed growth. A major hurdle for teams to overcome during this process is the belief that they must provide special education as the early intervention. The issue or problem here is that they are stating that the child has a disability. They are not stating on the report, under qualification, that they "just want to help."

A child cannot be qualified as disabled simply because a family cannot or will not create the needed experiences, exposure, expectations and then support these with practice. When the presenting problem does not represent a disability, the problem is better solved through working with the families or communities to create the needed experiences, exposure, expectations and practice. This is not a value judgment. Many families are doing their very best to provide food and shelter.

The Fourth Group: The Disproportionality Increases

These are the most problematic categories for Black/African American Students

- Intellectual Disability
- Emotional/Behavioral Disability

Intellectual Disability

There is a long and disturbing history of over qualification of Black/African American students as students with intellectual disabilities. There are court cases that address this problem, to the extent that the bulk of California has rules against the usage of IQ tests with Black/African American students. If your district has this problem, a great deal of work is needed to understand what belief systems and acculturation issues are feeding into this problem.

The following two slides let you know how extreme the disproportionality is for Black/African American students in the areas of intellectual disability and emotional/behavioral disability. This helps all of us understand how important it is to improve our results in these areas.

Report to Congress on Disproportionality

Using data from the U.S. Department of Education, analyses suggest that Black children are 2.88 times more likely than White children to be labeled as having mental retardation and 1.92 times more likely to be labeled as having an emotional/behavioral disorder (Losen & Orfield, 2002). Research suggests that unconscious racial bias, stereotypes, inequitable implementation of discipline policies, and practices that are not culturally responsive may contribute to the observed patterns of identification and placement for many minority students."

Information from the *Twenty-fourth Annual Report to Congress on the Implementation of the Individuals with Disabilities Education Act (IDEA)* (U.S. Department of Education, 2002), available at: http://www2.ed.gov/about/reports/annual/osep/2002/index.html

Education Week on Disproportionality

"... African-American students were nearly or greater than twice as likely as white students to be classified with emotional or intellectual disabilities

In other words, there are kids who are placed in these programs because educators either don't want to deal with them, don't know how to deal with them, or don't know how to be responsive to them.

Scholars generally don't blame racial disproportionality in special education on outright discrimination. Instead, they say it typically derives from systemic flaws within a school or district's instructional culture that allow for some disadvantaged students to fall through the cracks."

Keeping Special Ed in Proportion, by Anthony Rebora, available at:
http://www.edweek.org/tsb/articles/2011/10/13/01disproportion.h05.html

Emotional/Behavioral Disability

As with Intellectual Disabilities, this is a problem that has existed for a long period of time and many districts are struggling to address this issue. This issue creates a great deal of tension within staff members, given that there is often blame and belief system problems. Furthermore, it is rare to find a staff member who is comfortable with discussing what might be the core issues around this problem. As quoted in this book, there are issues related to staff understanding the needs of these students in order to be responsive instead of reactionary, and some staff do not want to deal with these issues due to fear of being criticized or accused of racism. The research does not indicate that outright racism is the issue, but instead unconscious racial bias. The authors believe that this is related to how each of us is acculturated and what each of us believes. If your district does not have over identification in this area, then examine what you are doing and keep doing it. If your district does have over identification in this area, then some staff are going to need to find the courage to have very difficult discussions. Solutions start with the identification of the underlying problems.

The Final Eligibility Category: The Category that Creates Tremendous Stress Within Teams

- Specific Learning Disability

There is research to support that the vast majority of the children who are incorrectly identified for special education are identified within the category of Specific Learning Disability.

This is a category that was, more or less, created for the special education world. It is the only category that greatly increased beyond population change from 1975 to 2004, when the special education population in the United States peaked between 2000 and 2004. It is the main category to decrease in size since 2004. The SLD category tripled in numbers from 1975 to 2004, eventually being the category in which roughly 50% of all special education students were qualified. Interestingly enough, the decrease in this category started with the federal law that included the usage of RTI qualification.

All Rights reserved by Steve Gill and Ushani Nanayakkara

It is easy to see the decrease in the SLD category aligning with the increased usage of RTI within the school systems. At last check, SLD now represents roughly 39.2% of all students qualified for special education (This was written in 2016 looking at the most current OSEP published data).

Below are a series of quotes that Steve uses when providing training in this area. For each quote I am providing additional information. These quotes provide a lot to think about and are followed by ways to mitigate these concerns.

> Dr. Carnine (University of Oregon) testifying to the Senate
> - "Moving to a response to intervention model can dramatically reduce the long-term failure that is often associated with the IQ-achievement discrepancy formula. 70 to 90 percent of the most at risk children in Kindergarten through 2nd grade can be brought to the average range with effective instruction."

The research into well-implemented RTI, or Tiered Intervention, has shown that many students who would have previously qualified under SLD have been appropriately served (and have better long term outcomes) through interventions implemented within the general education setting. Also, as noted in the law, students are not supposed to be found eligible when their needs can be met within the general education setting or if there is a lack of appropriate instruction in reading or math.

> Dr. Torgeson from Florida
> - "Within 1 year following the intervention, 40% of the children were found to be no longer in need of special education services."
> This was only 8 weeks of intervention at 2 hours per day and the children were labeled "with severe reading disabilities…"

Whether looking at this research or the research around the Lindamood Bell approach, it is easy to see that short-term intensive interventions focused on the specific needs of the children show that many children do not have disabilities, but instead, are casualties of our system. The research noted above was with children considered to have "severe reading disabilities." Studies show that similar methods with students who would be considered to have mild reading disabilities have results of up to

80% no longer needing special education services. Think about the implications. What if 50% of all students in special education (taking the 80% of SLD students and adding a small error rate in the other categories that are "soft") do not actually have disabilities and actually just need intensive interventions?

WAC 392-172A-03020

"(3) Each school district must ensure that:

(a) Assessments and other evaluation materials used to assess a student:

(i) **Are selected and administered so as not to be discriminatory on a racial or cultural basis;**

(ii) Are provided and administered in the student's native language or other mode of communication and in the form most likely to yield accurate information on what the student knows and can do academically, developmentally, and functionally unless it is clearly not feasible to so provide or administer;"

As noted in the law school teams are supposed to have practices that do not lead to discrimination, and school teams are supposed to evaluate the student in the student's native language (or using a format most likely to yield accurate information). Yet, we know that our practices lead to the use of the SLD category at rates higher for our ELL students (sometimes much higher) and Black/African American students according to OSEP data. And, for our language learners we are saying that these students have a disability in reading, math or written language in a language they are just learning (unless we have proof that they had the same learning issues in their prior country when applicable).

All Rights reserved by Steve Gill and Ushani Nanayakkara

WAC 392-172A-03040

"(2)(a) A student **must not be determined to be eligible** for special education services **if** the determinant factor is:

(i) **Lack of appropriate instruction in reading**, based upon the state's grade level standards;

(ii) **Lack of appropriate instruction in math**; or

(iii) **Limited English proficiency**; and

(b) If the student does not otherwise meet the eligibility criteria including presence of a disability, adverse educational impact and need for specially designed instruction.

(3) In interpreting evaluation data for the purpose of determining eligibility for special education services, each school district must:

(a) Draw upon information from a variety of sources, including aptitude and achievement tests, parent input, and teacher recommendations, as well as information about the student's physical condition, social or cultural background, and adaptive behavior; and

(b) Ensure that information obtained from all of these sources is documented and carefully considered."

This law has several issues that apply to evaluation. School teams are supposed to rule-out lack of appropriate instruction in reading and math. However, how does a student get appropriate instruction in reading and math if that instruction is not provided in their native language? School teams are supposed to factor in social and cultural background yet in most evaluations it is very difficult to find evidence of this done with fidelity. Is there appropriate instruction in reading and/or math if less than 50% of the students are passing the state tests? 40%? 30%? 20%?

You have seen the problems and concerns, now what?

All Rights reserved by Steve Gill and Ushani Nanayakkara

We suggest introspection, examining data, using a process, monitoring the results, and adjusting to meet goals that represent proportionality. This is not about putting fewer kids into special education (if your numbers already make sense), and it is also not about putting more kids in either (we are already over identifying). It is about qualifying the right kids. This is hard to do, unless you and your team work to identify the issues and address them.

Chapter 9: Face Validity

The purpose of this chapter is to help staff work together to set a minimum standard, one that can be built upon. We have put together a list of possible data/documentation that can facilitate reaching face validity for each of these categories. Each team will need to make sure to examine their state laws for alignment with these suggestions and then work with their district staff. If it is the district staff working on this, then they would need to work with their School Psychologists, Speech and Language Pathologists, Occupational Therapists, and Physical Therapists. This work can help to reduce some of the variation in qualification rates seen across districts (like the earlier chart that showed the variation in qualification rates across school buildings in one district).

Face Validity is being used in this context to indicate whether or not a person who is trained in evaluating students for special education could look at the evaluation report, and, after quickly reading the report conclude that the qualification appears to be valid. This person would not know the student personally, but upon reading the report would believe that the team had completed a thoughtful and thorough process that is solidly based upon data documented in the report.

Important Related Information:

Important note: Some states use 13 eligibility categories and some use 14 eligibility categories, some split Deaf from Hard of Hearing, some split Other Health Impaired into two groups, some split Blind from Visually Impaired, and some do not. Therefore, your state categories may be slightly different.

Also, some states talk about "need special education and related services" and some talk about "need specially designed instruction" and Washington falls in the latter. On a side note, the "need special education and related services" has an error in the writing, given a student does not "need" related services in order to qualify for special education.

Important Note: A comprehensive evaluation requires that the team considers the data and allows it to lead them. There are numerous legal cases in which districts were found to have not completed a comprehensive evaluation, because they only looked at characteristics commonly found within the disability category that they had presumed from the beginning of the process. The following lists will help address minimum standards once a comprehensive evaluation has been completed and is not meant to limit the scope of any evaluation.

Hearing Impairment

Obtain or document during the evaluation process:

1) Documentation of a hearing impairment or of fluctuating hearing from a qualified provider.
2) Testing and/or measurement in all areas of proposed service eligibility.
3) General education input that is supportive of eligibility.
4) Explanation and description of adverse impact and the need for specially designed instruction (SDI) as related to this specific data.

Deafness

Obtain or document during the evaluation process:

1) Documentation from a qualified provider that the student has deafness.
2) Testing and/or measurement in all areas of proposed service eligibility.
3) General education input that is supportive of eligibility. If not possible, documented explanation of why it is not possible.
4) Explanation and description of adverse impact and the need for specially designed instruction (SDI) as related to this specific data.

Visual Impairment (Including Blindness)

Obtain or document during the evaluation process:

1) Documentation from a qualified provider that the student has a visual impairment or blindness.
2) Testing and/or measurement in all areas of proposed service eligibility.
3) General education input that is supportive of eligibility.
4) Explanation and description of adverse impact and the need for specially designed instruction (SDI) as related to this specific data.

Orthopedic Impairment

Obtain or document during the evaluation process:

1) Documentation of a related medical condition that meets the WAC (or your state) criteria by a qualified provider.
2) Testing and/or measurement in all areas of proposed service eligibility.
3) General education input that is supportive of eligibility.
4) Specially designed instruction (SDI) that includes services from an OT and/or PT.
5) Explanation and description of adverse impact and the need for SDI as related to this specific data.

Traumatic Brain Injury

Obtain or document during the evaluation process:

1) Documentation of an injury, from a qualified practitioner, that meets the WAC (or your state) criteria.
2) Testing and/or measurement in all areas of proposed service eligibility.
3) General education input that is supportive of eligibility, or if that is not possible an explanation of why it is not possible.

4) Explanation and description of adverse impact and the need for specially designed instruction (SDI) as related to this specific data.

Deaf-Blind

Obtain or document during the evaluation process:

1. Documentation from a qualified provider that the student has deafness and blindness.
2. Testing and/or measurement in all areas of proposed service eligibility.
3. If available, general education input that is supportive of eligibility (if not available, explain why it is not available).
4. Explanation and description of adverse impact and the need for specially designed instruction (SDI) as related to this specific data.

Multiple Disabilities

Obtain or document during the evaluation process:

1) The documentation of two (or more) of the 14 disability categories, using the guidance from your district or state regarding the categories that logically could fit together.
2) These students are usually severely impacted students and are usually in the most restrictive of settings due to their significant needs. Provide written documentation that supports this decision.
3) A description of how the impairments are "the combination of which causes such severe educational needs that they cannot be accommodated in special education programs solely for one of the impairments." This is WAC (Washington Administrative Code – The Special Education Section) wording, you need to examine the wording of your state laws.
4) If available, general education input that is supportive of eligibility (if not available, explain why it is not available).

5) Explanation and description of adverse impact and the need for specially designed instruction (SDI) as related to this specific data.

Autism

Obtain or document during the evaluation process:

1) Documentation from a qualified provider that the student has Autism, Asperger's, PDD or equivalent. Check your state requirements and note the DSM changes and shifts in the related definitions.
2) Test and/or measurement data in all areas noted as concerns (usually academic, social, behavioral, communication as a minimum).
3) Communication (especially pragmatics) must be addressed, given that this is one of the core diagnostic features in an autism diagnosis.
4) More extensive observational documentation to assist with understanding the environmental issues impacting the student. Research on students with autism indicates many issues can be solved by changes to the environment and/or rituals within the environment.
5) General education input that is supportive of eligibility. If not possible, provide an explanation.
6) Explanation and description of adverse impact and the need for specially designed instruction (SDI) as related to this specific data.

Intellectual Disability

Obtain or document during the evaluation process:

Important Note: Check your state laws regarding numbers 1 and 2. Some states use 70 as a standard score, some use 75, and some use the phrase "significantly sub average."

All Rights reserved by Steve Gill and Ushani Nanayakkara

1) Intellectual test data that is <u>approximately</u> a standard score of 70 or below (or -2.0 SDs). Note, students can be qualified with scores slightly higher when the overall data is supportive.
2) Adaptive behavior data that is <u>approximately</u> a standard score of 70 or below (or -2.0 SDs).
3) Academic data that is supportive of an intellectual disability and a need for specially designed instruction (SDI). This is not a requirement of eligibility, but it's hard to defend a case without this.
4) Areas of SDI should be reflective of a student with an intellectual disability (e.g., learning to write a sentence versus learning to write for different audiences).
5) General education input that is supportive of eligibility. If that is not possible, provide an explanation of why it is not possible.
6) Explanation and description of adverse impact and need for SDI as related to this specific data.

Emotional Behavioral Disability

Obtain or document during the evaluation process:

1) Behavioral ratings that are significantly outside the norm.
2) Documentation of in-school behaviors that are significantly outside the norm (and have occurred over a long period of time).
3) Explanation of how one (or more) of the noted A-E (see WAC- Washington Administrative Code- Special Education Section) are documented using the noted data. Or use your state's special education language for this category.
4) If available, general education input that is supportive of qualification (if that is not available, explain why it is not available).
5) Explanation and description of adverse impact and the need for specially designed instruction (SDI) as related to this specific data.

Other Health Impairment

Obtain or document during the evaluation process:

1) Documentation of a medical condition by a qualified provider.
2) Documentation of an adverse educational impact directly and logically related to the noted medical condition.
3) Test and/or measurement data in area of specially designed instruction (SDI) that is supportive of eligibility.
4) General education input that is supportive of eligibility.
5) Explanation and description of adverse impact and the need for SDI as related to this specific data.

Speech or Language Impairment

Obtain or document during the evaluation process:

1) Test and/or measurement (formal and informal) data in the area(s) of eligibility.
2) Information from the general education setting (for preschool children from appropriate activities) that includes specific examples of this area of eligibility that support decision(s) made (i.e., areas of eligibility if eligible).
3) Rule out cultural, English language issues and/or poverty issues.
4) Explanation and description of adverse impact and the need for specially designed instruction (SDI) as related to this specific data.

Developmentally Delayed

Obtain or document during the evaluation process:

1) Test scores that meet the WAC numerical criteria (or your state's criteria) for each area of qualification. The qualification areas must be the noted DD areas:

All Rights reserved by Steve Gill and Ushani Nanayakkara

Cognitive Development, Communication Development, Physical Development, Social or Emotional Development, and/or Adaptive Development.
2) General education input that is supportive of eligibility (when applicable). Or, for preschool children, in appropriate activities.
3) Explanation and description of adverse impact and the need for specially designed instruction (SDI) as related to this specific data.

Specific Learning Disability

Obtain or document during the evaluation process:

1) Academic testing, almost always formal and standardized. RTI data if RTI qualification is formally adopted by your district in accordance with state laws.
2) Intellectual testing data from at least one of the following:
    a. A recent test (within 6 months)
    b. Two past tests that have commensurate scores
    c. A solid explanation as to why only one past test is available if you are dealing with a re-evaluation and you are not re-instrumenting intelligence testing
    d. RTI methodology if following appropriate legal requirements.
3) Documentation of Severe Discrepancy. If professional judgment is used, it must document a severe discrepancy and use the format outlined in your state laws, or RTI methodology if following appropriate legal requirements.
4) Documentation of classroom observation (in addition to other observations).
5) General education input that is supportive of eligibility.
6) Explanation and description of adverse impact and the need for specially designed instruction (SDI) as related to this specific data.

All Rights reserved by Steve Gill and Ushani Nanayakkara

Appendix A: Sources of Information Regarding Problems in Qualification

Many of you will be facing a variety of challenges in discussing the appropriate students to evaluate for special education services.

Each of these is directly quoted from the source noted. The source of the information for the following excerpts is listed first. Please refer to the source for further information.

ChildTrends

Child Trends Databank. (2014). Learning disabilities. Available at:
http://www.childtrends.org/?indicators=learning-disabilities

> *Differences by Parental Education In 2013, children who had a parent with a Bachelor's degree or higher were less likely to have a learning disability than those with parents who had only a high school diploma or some college…*
>
> *Children in poverty and in families that receive public assistance are more likely to be identified as having a learning disability.*

Important Note: Rate of identification does not equal rate of disability. Think about this over time, it is a huge issue in our field.

Education Week

Keeping Special Ed in Proportion, by Anthony Rebora, available at:
http://www.edweek.org/tsb/articles/2011/10/13/01disproportion.h05.html

> ... African-American students were nearly or greater than twice as likely as white students to be classified with emotional or intellectual disabilities
>
> In other words, there are kids who are placed in these programs because educators either don't want to deal with them, don't know how to deal with them, or don't know how to be responsive to them.
>
> Scholars generally don't blame racial disproportionality in special education on outright discrimination. Instead, they say it typically derives from systemic flaws within a school or district's instructional culture that allow for some disadvantaged students to fall through the cracks.

Report to Congress

Information from the *Twenty-fourth Annual Report to Congress on the Implementation of the Individuals with Disabilities Education Act (IDEA)* (U.S. Department of Education, 2002), available at:
http://www2.ed.gov/about/reports/annual/osep/2002/index.html

> Using data from the U.S. Department of Education, analyses suggest that Black children are 2.88 times more likely than White children to be labeled as having mental retardation and 1.92 times more likely to be labeled as having an emotional/behavioral disorder (Losen & Orfield, 2002). Research suggests that unconscious racial bias, stereotypes, inequitable implementation of discipline policies, and practices that are not culturally responsive may contribute to the observed patterns of identification and placement for many minority students.

NASP

NASP Communiqué, Vol. 38, #1, September 2009

Multicultural Affairs, Confronting Inequity in Special Education, Part I: Understanding the Problem of Disproportionality, by Amanda L. Sullivan, Elizabeth A'Vant, John Baker, Daphne Chandler, Scott Graves, Edward McKinney, & Tremaine Sayles:

> Black students, particularly those identified as mentally retarded or emotionally disabled, have been consistently overrepresented for more than 3 decades. Native American students are also persistently overrepresented in special education nationally, and while the same is not true for Latino students, they are often overrepresented at the state and district levels where their enrollment is highest.
>
> Special education identification patterns vary both between and within states. For instance, risk for Black students identified as mentally retarded is more than 14 times that of their White peers in some states while risk is nearly equivalent in others.
>
> The disproportionality literature tends to focus on the disability categories of mental retardation, learning disabilities, and emotional disabilities, as these are the high-incidence disabilities and constitute over 63% of students eligible for special education (U.S. Department of Education [USDOE], 2009). These are also widely regarded as "judgmental" categories because of relatively vague federal and state disability definitions that necessitate a high degree of professional judgment in making normative comparisons to determine eligibility (Klingner et al., 2005). This has led many to question the validity of these diagnoses as true disabilities and the likelihood of misidentification, particularly in light of the wide variation in identification rates across states and districts. In contrast, diagnoses in the low-incidence categories are rarely challenged because of their

physical/medical bases, and because disproportionality is not generally observed in these categories.

Center for Public Education

This examination of special education was prepared for the Center for Public Education by Ulrich Boser, October 15, 2009, available at:

Found at: www.centerforpubliceducatio.org

The complete URL is listed below:

http://www.centerforpubliceducation.org/Main-Menu/Evaluating-performance/Special-education-At-a-glance/Special-education-A-better-perspective-full-report.html

> *The disparities between whites and some minorities in special education appear mostly in the categories with the most subjective eligibility criteria, such as "mild mental retardation" or "specific learning disabilities." Many believe the disproportionate representation is due to misconceptions about race and culture, and that black and Hispanic children are more likely to be misidentified as disabled (Education Week 2004, National Research Council 2002).*
>
> *For instance, Matthew Ladner and Christopher Hammons argue that race plays an enormously important role in how students are identified as disabled (Ladner and Hammons, 2001). In a study in the book Rethinking Special Education for a New Century, they found that in districts with a predominantly black faculty, there was a reduction in minority student enrollment in special education services by three to four times. "Race," they concluded, "impacts special education rates far more than any other variable.*

University of Texas at Austin

Education and Transition to Adulthood, Information on Learning Disabilities, available at: http://www.utexas.edu/cola/etag/Related%20Sites/Learning-Disabilities.php

Although the research focus has primarily been on the disproportionate labeling of racial minorities with LD, the research team found that differences in the rates of being labeled are more dramatic by socioeconomic status (SES) than by race. The odds of being labeled with LD are much higher among low SES than high SES high school students, regardless of whether the student is black or white. In fact, low SES white high school students are as likely as low SES black or Hispanic high school students to be labeled with LD, but much greater proportions of racial minorities are in that high-risk low SES group.

In contrast to black and white high school students, high SES Hispanic high school students are as likely as low SES Hispanic high school students to be labeled with LD. The team found that disproportionate labeling of Hispanic students with learning disabilities in high school is attributable to the over-labeling of language minorities.

The team also found that students attending higher poverty schools are actually less likely to be labeled with LD, and that systematic differences in academic achievement by SES, race, and linguistic status are a major factor in disproportionality.

Articles on Culturally Responsive Mental Health Interventions

Jones, J.M. (Ed.) (2009). *The psychology of multiculturalism in schools: A primer for practice, training, and research*. Bethesda, MD: National Association of School Psychologists.

Jones, J.M. (2017). Culturally-responsive collective impact teams: An interdisciplinary vision for the future. In E. Lopez, S. Nahari, and S. Proctor

(Eds.). *Handbook of Multicultural School Psychology: An interdisciplinary perspective, 2nd Ed.* Mahwah, NJ : Erlbaum.

Jones, J.M. (2013). Family, school, and community partnerships. In D. Shriberg, S.Y. Song, A.H. Miranda, and K.M. Radliff (Eds.) *School Psychology and Social Justice: Conceptual foundations and tools for practice.* New York, NY: Routledge Press.

Jones, J.M. (2011) Culturally Diverse Families: Enhancing Home-School Relationships. In A. Canter, L. Paige, L. & S. Shaw (Eds.) *Helping children at home and school- III.* Bethesda, MD: National Association of School Psychologists.

Appendix B: Recommended Books

Virginia Collier and Wayne Thomas:

- Dual Language Education for a Transformed World
- Educating English Language Learners for a Transformed World

Carol Dweck

- Mindset: The New Psychology of Success

Steve Gill and Ushani Nanayakkara

- The Ell Critical Data Process: Distinguishing Between Disability and Language Acquisition
- Evaluating ELL Students for the Possibility of Special Education

John Hattie

- Visible Learning: A Synthesis of over 800 Meta-Analyses Related to Achievement

Anthony Muhammed

- Overcoming the Achievement Gap Trap

Robert Rhodes, Salvador Hector Ochoa, and Samuel Ortiz

- Assessing Culturally and Linguistically Diverse Students

Appendix C: Training by Steve Gill

Steve Gill is available to provide all-day training sessions on ELL and special education issues, and is in the process of creating an all-day training centered around the content of this book. For more information, contact Steve at: Stevegill2011@yahoo.com.

Steve Gill Biography

Steve's first job in education, before he became a school psychologist, was as a driver's education teacher. Steve had a wonderful opportunity to study school psychology and work at the university, so he followed that path. Steve started his career as a school psychologist in a district with a large ELL population. There he realized how little he had learned about language learners prior to this experience. Over the years, he completed graduate work in ELL studies, eventually creating the ELL Critical Data Process. As of writing this, Steve has trained over 6,000 educators on the process across more than 200 school districts in multiple states. Steve and Ushani (Steve's wife and co-author) have three books for sale on Amazon.com. The first book, *The ELL Critical Data Process,* is a resource for learning professionals for determining whether more interventions are needed or if a special education referral is a reasonable option. Their second book, *Evaluating ELL Students for the Possibility of Special Education Qualification* went into print in September of 2015, and focuses on the special education evaluation process for language learners and how to potentially achieve appropriate identification rates. Steve is currently working in the Kent School District as the ESA Coach (coaching school psychologists, speech and language pathologists, occupational therapists, and physical therapists on special education processes and issues).

All Rights reserved by Steve Gill and Ushani Nanayakkara

Brief Overview of the 1-Day Training Program

Section 1:

The first section of the training covers background issues, problems, laws, and research needed to assist staff in addressing the belief systems of others, and their own belief systems that are impacting the progress in this field. The content focuses on understanding the relationship between acculturation, belief systems, practices and results.

Section 2:

The second section of the training addresses how children qualify for special education services with a focus on ELL specific issues that arise during qualification. This includes how to reduce the problems and core issues that lead to disproportionality, while breaking down the problem to three main areas of qualification.

Section 3:

The third section focuses on training those in attendance on how to complete the ELL Critical Data Process. This is the process created by Steve that helps staff to gather the most critical data, follow a structured process, and create a product that helps them to see whether more interventions are needed or if a special education referral is a reasonable option. The ELL Critical Data Process brings key staff members to the table and structures the discussions so that a student's needs are better understood.

Other Training Options

Steve often adds an additional ½ day to include a training on the Preschool Version of the ELL Critical Data Process and an additional hour for discussion of real cases.

Steve also provides each of the sections above as individual trainings at state conferences or for local districts, depending upon their requests.

All Rights reserved by Steve Gill and Ushani Nanayakkara

Steve is in the process of developing a 1-day training to support the content of this book and a 2-3 hour training for local districts that focuses on this process (for districts who are already using the ELL Critical Data Process). These sessions will be available for the 2017/2018 school year. Also, there is the option to combine this new training to create a 2-day training event that would cover the two ELL Critical Data Process trainings and the training for the content from this book.

Feedback on Trainings, Process, and Books

Diversity and Social Justice Training Feedback

"I'd like to take this opportunity to thank you again for sharing your expertise with our members on March 21st at the Diversity and Social Justice Conference. As you can see from the feedback below, the participants were filled with insights and inspiration that will affect their practice. We appreciate your consideration to return as a speaker as we plan future offerings. Thank you!! C."

Feedback on Steve Gill's presentations – "Special Ed Qualification Issues with a Focus on ELL issues" and "The ELL Critical Data Process"

- All good! Great useful information and perspective from very knowledgeable, expert/professional – could be two day training☺.
- Steve and Jeff were great, both content and delivery!
- Even though I do not teach a large number of ELL students, the things I learned can be directly applied to all students, regardless of background.
- I will use/take the information from the SPED/ELL breakout sessions in teaching, assessing, evaluating and potentially referring – or NOT – kids for SPED.

District Training Feedback:

"When you sit through one of Steve's Data Matrix trainings, it becomes extremely clear how much school districts have lacked the expertise and methods for carrying out referrals and evaluations on students who are English Language Learners. I personally learned more in the 2-hour session about English Language Learners than I ever did in graduate school or my own practice. His work is thorough, eye-opening, and most importantly, practical." AG, School Psychologist

"Steve uses research based content and district data in his presentation with both care and humor. He is conscientious to both recognize the passion of educators, while working to move them forward in their practice of evaluating students from second language backgrounds. This is such an important topic for staff and Steve's work is critical in helping to move our district forward in this area. The protocol that Steve has developed should be required of any team evaluating an ELL student for possible special education eligibility." KH, Asst. Director of Special Education

"Steve's presentation was clear, concise and built on foundational principals of Special Education, Civil Rights, and the science of language learning and was immediately relevant to the real work that we do every day as school practitioners facing complicated questions. His training and material was the catalyst that launched our district on a path toward more informed interventions for culturally and linguistically diverse students." BC, Special Services Coordinator

"I'm sorry it has taken me so long to thank you for your wonderful ELL Pre-referral Presentation for us here in Battle Ground. I have heard so many positive comments about your presentation and the protocol/matrix that you have created.

All Rights reserved by Steve Gill and Ushani Nanayakkara

Everyone I spoke to, which included school psychologists, Reading Specialists and ELL Specialists said they thought the protocol/matrix was the best they had ever seen and should be used for all students.

You presented such a wealth of information and made so many excellent comments! One thing I heard over and over was that everyone should have this training. They said they had gained valuable information that has changed how they view ELL students' language abilities and how they would assess ELL students in the future.

You are providing such a valuable service to the districts around the state and to our ELL students and families. We really are lucky to have your expertise.

Thank you for making the effort to come to our district and share your vast knowledge on the ELL Pre-referral process for ELL students."

JM, ELL Coordinator

"Your book is wonderful--a very much needed resource in an area of great need. Thanks for sending us a copy! Although we are not specialists in special education, we have done enough work with doctoral graduates who are bilingual special ed. experts to know that your book has a system for appropriate assessment that is very much more comprehensive than anything else we have seen to date. Wow, you have reached many educators in the state of Washington through this training and providing this book to them! And you can indeed be proud of your work, reducing the number of English learners assessed as needing special education services, across the state of Washington." VC, Professor, Researcher, Author

"Dear …,

I wanted to write to you to tell you how invaluable Steve Gill's training was for our District yesterday. He presented to 63 staff members who sit on our building Guidance Teams: Principals, Deans of Students, School Counselors, School Psychologists, and

Speech/Language Pathologists. He presented for a full day on ELL and Special Education and then remained for extra time to offer examples and specific guidance for the process he has developed to our school psychologists. He was a compelling speaker, he easily engaged and held the attention of all of the participants. He cited research and used data throughout. He used our own District data to inform us about how we are addressing dually identified students (ELL/IDEA) in our District providing us a road map for improvement. I want to thank you for allowing Steve to bring this important knowledge and practice to other Districts.

Thanks so much, on behalf of our staff, and especially, our students."

SW, Special Education Director

"Thank you so very much for sharing such a wonderful presentation with Eastmont and our neighbors. Your insight is so valuable to our advocacy for diverse learners. I'm looking forward to teaming with our Special Education department to ensure students are appropriately served. You're responsible for bridging our services. What a huge benefit for our student!

Your wit, knowledge, and expertise made for such a worthwhile experience for all of us. Thank You!

We really appreciate your time and efforts."

AD, ELL Director

Made in the USA
Columbia, SC
15 February 2020